# AWAKEN YOUR WEALTH

# AWAKEN
# YOUR
# WEALTH

### CREATING A PACT
### *to* OPTIMIZE YOUR MONEY
### *and* YOUR LIFE

JULIE MARIE MURPHY, CFP®

BEYOND YOUR WILDEST DREAMS, LLC
CHICAGO

# AWAKEN YOUR WEALTH

## CREATING A PACT *to* OPTIMIZE YOUR MONEY *and* YOUR LIFE

© 2019 Julie Marie Murphy, CFP*

ISBN: 978-0-9801133-1-0 paperback
ISBN-13: 978-0-9801133-2-7 eBook
Library of Congress Control Number: 2019939609

Cover Design by:

Gabriele Wilson

Printed in the United States of America

# WHAT *IS* THE PACT™?

**P:** Picturing Yourself

**A:** Accepting Reality and Awakening

**C:** Choosing to Change

**T:** Taking Action

## DEDICATION

I dedicate this book to all the little loves in my life. You bring so much happiness into my world and are my babies forever:

Timmy, Bridget, Mary Kate, and Michael.

## THE PEOPLE INCLUDED IN THIS BOOK

You will find numerous personal stories throughout *Awaken Your Wealth!* Over the course of my career, I've been richly blessed with a colorful mosaic of clients and supportive team members. I'm continually amazed at the honesty, depth, and integrity of my clients and co-workers. Now it is my pleasure to share with you all of what we have learned together. To protect their privacy, the stories used throughout *Awaken Your Wealth!* are composites of client histories and actual experiences represented by fictitious names. The case studies are based on the ways in which hundreds of people have navigated and utilized the PACT system, yet they do not apply to any one, specific, particular, identifiable individual.

I understand and value the power of personal stories and believe we learn most effectively through our own stories and those of others. These selected vignettes capture the heart of this book and will be very helpful to you as you make your own PACT with your financial future (i.e.: Picturing Yourself, Accepting Reality and Awakening, Choosing to Change, and Taking Action). I know you will be able to relate to many of these stories. By viewing wealth building through the lens of other people's experiences, your eyes will open to the infinite possibilities of a new reality for yourself, one filled with happiness, quality of life, prosperity, abundance, and inner peace.

Securities offered through LPL Financial, Member FINRA/SIPC, Financial planning and advisory services through JMC Wealth Management, Inc., a registered investment advisor and separate entity from LPL Financial.

# TABLE OF CONTENTS

*"Man. Because he sacrifices his health in order to make money.*
*Then he sacrifices money to recuperate his health.*
*And then he is so anxious about the future*
*that he does not enjoy the present;*
*the result being that he does not live in the present or the future;*
*he lives as if he is never going to die,*
*and then dies having never really lived."*

**~THE DALAI LAMA**

**CHAPTER 1**

# MONEY

*Money is only a tool. It will take you wherever you wish,*
*but it will not replace you as the driver.*
*~AYN RAND*

Money problems are not new. People around the world have always faced serious financial issues. But today, the statistics are, in a word, shocking! CNN ran an article titled, "76% of Americans Are Living Paycheck-to-Paycheck." Surprised? About three-quarters of all Americans live literally dependent upon the arrival of that next paycheck, without back-up emergency savings, unable to handle a sudden job loss, a medical crisis, or financial surprises of any kind. This CNN piece (by Angela Johnson, Money.CNN.com., June 24, 2013) reported on a national survey of adults where half of those polled had less than a three-month cushion, and 25 percent had less than $100 in savings, while half had less than $800 put aside for a rainy day.

Where credit is concerned, the story gets even worse. An online survey conducted between November 2-4, 2015, within the United States by Harris Poll for NerdWallet.com (reported by Erin El Issa), found that about 40 percent of all Americans carry credit card debt. The typical debt per American household is $5,700, with the average credit card balance among households is around $15,760. Much of the world has also followed suit.

Debt rises with increased income. Consumers making four-, five-, and even six-figure incomes find that after paying off debts and taking care of housing, car, and child-care-related expenses, there simply isn't enough money left over for saving. This is true for each and every socioeconomic stratum. We are a world living and spending for the moment, not saving for retirement, teetering one tiny step away from financial disaster.

It's all an absolute mess—creating chaos that I see up-close and personal every day as an independent wealth advisor. I feel the universal pain in this vicious cycle of overspending and the resulting volumes of debt: credit cards, car, and various other kinds of debts. For years, I contributed to the statistics, burdened by college loans, helping out family members in need, and subconsciously terrified by my parents' fear-based belief system that there would never be enough money to keep us afloat. I was actually quite good at creating income and accumulating wealth. However, for many years, no matter how much I made, it slipped through my fingers as quickly as it arrived. Something always "came up."

## An Energy Shift

We are all comprised of energy. Our bodies are made up of energy. Everything we come in contact with is energy, and, in fact, our entire existence on this earth and beyond is made up of fields of energy. Money is energy too—stored energy. The key to financial success is changing our relationship to money. We need to harness and shift our energy, focusing on what we want, rather than on what we do not want. You must transfer attention to what will work for you, emphasizing the positive result and ignoring the obstacles. This mindset allows you to shift forward, out of where you have been to where you want to go.

When it comes to what I'll deem "money think," we duplicate the attitudes and lessons learned from our families of origin, eventually repeating the sins of our mothers and fathers. For example, in my financial services business, a new client named Joan came to me wanting help reframing her economic forecast following a divorce. She was 48 and talked openly about her family, describing her parents as "loving, kind, and considerate people, totally committed to our family's well-being." However, she explained, "They were always, and still are, at war over money."

Her father often repeated the story of his family's curse: previous generations amassed significant fortunes only to lose them through bad investments, changes in the economy, or lavish overspending. Her father swore that would never happen to him or his family. He resolved to save more than he spent. In contrast, Joan's mother grew up in an affluent home where her wish was everyone else's command.

"I feel like I'm replaying their script, and I'm pretty sick of it," said Joan. "I married my high school sweetheart, who grew up to be a certified public accountant. Every word in his financial vocabulary was about providing for our children's education and saving for our retirement. My dialogue never changed, 'What about us? Isn't life for the living, now, in the moment?'" After 22 years, three children, $155,000 in savings and investments, $18,000 in debt, and a $250,000 mortgage, Joan and her husband gave up the daily battles and entered into a nasty divorce—fighting over every penny.

Joan and I worked together to take charge of and, in the process, drastically improve, her life, one building block at a time. At work, she signed up for matched savings and investment programs and opened savings accounts for each of her children. Using PACT as her blueprint, within six months, she had reframed her emotional and financial thinking, calling upon her own intuition and intelligence in the process.

## Money Makes the World Work

Money is one of the most difficult subjects to broach, a hot button for just about all of us. It is literally the energy that makes the world go round, propelling and supporting our lives. Just as we have relationships with our partners, children, and ourselves, we likewise live life with a long-term, ongoing financial connection.

What's *your* relationship with your money? Do you love it, hate it, need it, want it, make it, lose it, like it, save it, invest it, worship it, and fear it, or some combination thereof? Some of us just try to ignore our financial bottom line, hoping the money will be there when needed to make ends meet—and more. Others spend with abandon and suffer the consequences, never able to get ahead of the weight of debilitating debt and higher–than-average interest rates. Just thinking about money can be exhilarating and exasperating—at times, both!

Some people find it easier to talk about how often they have sex compared to talking about how much money they have coming in, going out, sitting in the bank, or invested for the future. Fortunately, once we understand money and our relationship with it, we can then be a fully present partner in our financial future. Let's face it: money is as critical a support system to our lifestyle and our overall health as the blood that courses through our veins!

## Creating a Working Solution

It's not unusual for people seeking to understand themselves better to turn to psychiatry as a career. When I needed to figure myself out, I turned to money management and financial planning. Having my own financial issues that needed resolution, I devoted my education and my life to learning everything I could about finance, economics, and money, first to help myself and then to help others. However, it was many years before I realized that by fixing my own dysfunctional money problems, I would also be dramatically improving every facet of my life. In the process of resolving my own issues, I created PACT, a four-step system that brings money matters and financial transformation out into the open—making this kind of transformation accessible to everyone.

After first using the PACT system for myself, I began applying its principles to my work with clients. At this point, PACT is thoroughly tried and true—and here for you. I did the extensive development, testing, and learning that formed its basis. However, PACT is actually all about you as an individual coming to terms with your conscious and subconscious monetary patterns. It is designed so that you, like myself and my clients, can create a new set of intentions that are aligned with your soul's deepest desires.

Now that I think about it, I've lived my whole life using PACT without realizing exactly what it was. I wanted to attend a BIG 10 school. I clearly stated my intention, and, in time, my mission was accomplished. I chose to earn my MBA from Notre Dame—done. I pictured myself starting my own company, and at age 22, I was a CEO. I wanted to write a book. I did, and it was well received. *Awaken Your Wealth! Creating a PACT to Optimize Your Money and Your Life* is my second one. I continuously stretch beyond any outer limits to find a way to achieve my goals. Today, this is exactly what I teach my clients, my workshop audiences, and my readers.

As a CERTIFIED FINANCIAL PLANNER™, I continually work through challenging situations to help people pursue their individual dreams. Using the PACT process, I can help everyone find a personalized path. I knew I was on to something very different as a financial planner. While my peers were struggling for referrals, I acquired hundreds upon hundreds of new clients annually, along with clients who have stayed with me through multiple generations. I don't sell products. I help people like you to confidently work towards pursuing the life they think they can only imagine.

After my first book, *The Emotion Behind Money: Building Wealth from the Inside Out*, was published, I had a real wake-up call when I spoke to a group of financial planners. All of them admitted that they did not understand anything I said. "Not a clue," laughed one highly respected, bearded, rotund gentleman, who had been in the business for more than 30 years. "Julie," he said, "I am not afraid to tell you that I cannot, for the life of me, figure out how picturing myself, accepting reality and awakening, and choosing to change the choices I make could have anything to do with money."

Everyone in the audience knew what "taking action" meant, but calling upon introspection, meditation, and diverse energy modalities to reframe clients' personal relationships with money—well, no way. They were essentially limited to the products they sold.

Fortunately, my speaking engagements introduced me to huge groups of general audiences at corporate "lunch and learn" seminars, in libraries, social groups, and clubs. The feedback was awesome: "Finally, someone in your field gets it." Now, I teach other financial planners how to use PACT so they, too, can help others in this very different, very effective way.

Upcoming chapters in this book will provide you with every PACT detail you need to live *your* life *your* way. PACT has transformed the lives of thousands from dysfunctional to functional. These adults have become fully aware of, and responsible for, their own financial decisions and choices. As I said, the life that was transformed first by PACT was my own. I am confident you will find PACT just as transformative as my clients have, and once you act upon it, you'll keep referring back to various chapters until you achieve the optimum relationship with your money.

# CHAPTER 2

# MY PROFESSIONAL JOURNEY

*Wealth is the ability to fully experience life.*
~HENRY DAVID THOREAU

I grew up Irish Catholic, the second oldest of 12 children, in Midlothian, Illinois, a working-class suburb of Chicago. I didn't really give much thought to what I wanted for my own life because everything revolved around doing what was best for the whole clan—even if it meant giving up personal dreams. I followed my parents' financial pattern: money was promised or spent before it was received.

My family struggled to stay afloat. I felt sorry for my youngest brothers and sisters because they just had hand-me-downs from siblings, extended family, and friends. With each one of our First Communions, my parents "borrowed" our gift money to help with the household expenses. My dad kept a notebook of every penny he ever garnished from his children, but we all accepted the fact that none of us would ever be repaid. It went towards the greater good of the household.

The most difficult part about being the second oldest—and an inherently responsible hard worker—was that everyone thought, or behaved as if, I'd provide what was needed. For many years, I did. I couldn't help it. If I had money in my pocket and my younger brother's jeans were frayed, we went shopping.

## Family Maintenance Was a Full-Time Job

From the time I could walk and talk, my job was taking care of my younger brothers and sisters. The 10 children born after me all arrived within 12 years. I often left my bed during the night to feed a crying baby and woke up in the morning in the recliner with the baby asleep on my shoulder. Routinely, I was startled awake to run around helping everyone get ready for school and out the door on time.

I had my first paying job at age six, delivering *The Penny Saver.* By the seventh grade, I added the *Chicago Tribune* and *Chicago Sun-Times* to my delivery route, before school and on weekends, for a huge pay raise. I was hooked and used my greatest talking and selling skills to raise money for school fundraisers and to enter every kind of contest. I won an Atari 2600 game, a beautiful, electric-blue Huffy 10-speed bicycle, and many small money prizes too. I learned to be direct and clear, to ask for exactly what I wanted from others, and, most often, to receive what I asked for. A spark was lit deep down within me. I knew early on that I wanted a different kind of life.

By the time I entered high school, buoyed by success after success, I still had no money saved. I spent it all or gave it to the family. Now I see my spending habits were based on the fearful belief that if I didn't buy what I wanted right then and there, I wouldn't have the money to buy it later. All I had known and experienced in my life was perpetual struggle. Living in survival mode, I developed a Scarcity mentality.

Little did I know how much this mindset affected everything in my life. My mother and I did the weekly grocery shopping together. When things were good, we received a treat. Moon Pies were everyone's favorite and perfect for us—since 12 came in a box. I remember Mom offering us a choice: save ours for our lunchboxes during the week or eat it immediately. We all ate them right away because we knew if we didn't, they would disappear.

Years later, one of my aunts told me how much she loved sharing the holidays with my family but had concerns because the 12 of us were like locusts swarming over the table. We piled food high on our plates, more than we could ever eat in one sitting, out of an ingrained fear of not having enough.

I did try to save some of my paper route and babysitting money, but it was very difficult. If there was no milk in the house, I went to the store, spent my money to buy a gallon, drank a glass or two, and the rest went to the other kids. At the time, I thought that was normal. What I did not realize was how this pattern would remain with me throughout my early adult years. I treated people to dinners out, trips, and gifts without ever expecting—or receiving—reciprocation. We loved each other, which was enough. However, a variety of "aha!" moments hit me hard, arriving in waves at different ages, foreshadowing the realization that there were many more options and much more to life than what I was experiencing.

## One Lesson Learned at a Time

Through trial and error, education, and research, I became my own economic experiment. I began with the numbers, taking a good look at my cash flow, where it came in and where it went out. That was certainly a wake-up call. Going through that process helped me understand why so many clients never wanted to open their mail, living in a world of denial with the hope that what they didn't know couldn't hurt them. The truth is, what we don't recognize and deal with can destroy us. Troubles are a lot like rabbits: they quickly multiply. It was when I began combining different modalities and techniques to shift my energy and support to the PACT system that my dysfunctional side, slowly but surely, began to disintegrate and then disappear.

As I said, all my life I had absolutely no problem creating a nice income. Holding on to it was the tricky part. As an adult, when I wanted to get to the next level in buying a new car or a condo, I didn't have enough cash on hand. Of course I didn't, since I continually spent on others, marching myself further into debt. I have subsequently learned that having an abundance of money made me feel uncomfortable. On the one hand, I believed money would solve all my problems, but on the other hand, whenever I had it, I self-sabotaged. This caused me to create more income to get out of debt, and the vicious cycle continued. I learned how to create cash windfalls but could not get that to work for me. Unfortunately, I saw myself as a debtor and needed to learn new ways of thinking and functioning, which we will discuss at length in chapter 5.

## Wake up and Decide

Facing reality often takes a loud wake-up call. In my junior year of college, I was expelled for poor performance—two semesters in a row! At the time, my emotional processing system was on overload. Not only was I trying to find my way in the world, I was also breaking away from the pack of 11 siblings. At the same time, my older sister was unmarried and pregnant, which was certainly not acceptable in a traditional Irish family. I was called upon by family members to find a solution, to make everything better for everyone.

I was being tested. Would I reveal what I really believed in, as opposed to what I "should" believe in? Would I continue to support, or not to support, those I loved, regardless of the fact that much of the hard times they faced they brought on themselves? This was a turning point in my life. It was my major opportunity to choose for myself. What did I really want? Who did I want in my life, blood-related or not? What did I want to create? I had to go after it, claim it, and get it right—and I did.

## Commitment to the Future

The truth was that I wasn't doing well in college because I wasn't living my own life. I clearly needed to make myself the priority. My brothers, sisters, father, and mother all depended upon me to help them out with everything that came up. I had to let them know, as nicely as possible, that if they had a problem, they needed to address it themselves as opposed to expecting Julie to go to battle for them. I needed to learn my way out of my personal dilemma. To begin, I contacted mentors—people I had counted on before for guidance when the going got tough. After one semester of being put on academic probation, I returned to school and eventually graduated with an A- cumulative average from the same university that had previously dropped me.

At age 22, I launched my own financial planning business without any guaranteed salary, continually building the mental and emotional muscles to succeed. I recognized immediately two common patterns in myself and my clients. The first was debt, debt, and more debt. Call it good debt, bad debt, or whatever debt; the bottom line is that debt makes you feel trapped because you're stuck in the muck and mire of your past choices.

The second pattern was that many people, myself included, could create and attract sizable salaries and some assets, but then could not hold on to the money they amassed. The money slipped through clients' fingers time and time again for various reasons. No matter the reasons, in the end, they came in seeking advice. I examined these two big financial milestones, releasing debt and creating sustainable wealth, and focused on how to help all of us create lasting, positive changes in these two basic areas of our lives.

JULIE'S GEMS:
# The Emotions of Real Estate

As I became more aware of other people's issues, I had to admit I was doing the same thing. Even as a married woman, mother, and business owner, I kept slipping backwards. This became very clear to me in 2013, right before my daughter Mary Kate was born, when I found myself frustrated at continuing to carry the expenses for a house I owned with my parents, across the street from the University of Notre Dame's football stadium.

After my father suffered a series of strokes in 2005, we took him to a Notre Dame football game, hoping to take his mind off of his medical condition. My grandfather played for Notre Dame in the 1940s, and my father is a walking encyclopedia on their football history. Making our way over to the stadium, we walked past a house with this sign: "For rent or sale to the right buyer." My dad became obsessed, called me daily, until we arranged to see the house, and we did finally make an offer to buy it.

Being a good daughter and wanting to extend his life with something he loved, living near Notre Dame during football season, I made it happen, including paying half of the down payment and overseeing all repairs that needed to be accomplished. Then I rented it out for the six to nine months my parents were not in town. In other words, I added another huge responsibility to my plate in the name of family.

We bought the house in South Bend, Indiana, in June 2006, and Dad hardly ever made it there. The emotional pay-off I sought, of helping him heal, never really materialized. After extensively paying out of pocket for it myself for years, I opted to rent it out in order to recover some of the cash.

I thought this decision would put the house situation in perfect alignment for me, but at the end of my pregnancy with MaryKate, the rental agent called to say that the current renters wanted to buy it at a reduced price. I wasn't interested in their offer, but remembered my personal motto: you either work things out, or they will act out. I made a firm decision and said, "If you locate the right buyer, I'll give you a finder's fee, and the higher the selling price, the more money you'll make." She quickly found the perfect buyer.

Not surprisingly, all kinds of emotions came up during the sale. My children and I attended our last football game of the season two weeks before the closing and loved being in the house. That made me realize I didn't only buy it for Dad; my heart was in it too. How could I have been so sure that I was supposed to sell the house I cared so much about? On top of that, being postpartum, I couldn't stop crying.

Deirdre Morgan, a heart-space expert, helped me clarify that I wasn't only grieving over selling the house. I was also crying over 40 years of my life where I put everyone else's needs before my own. Deep down, I knew she was right. I prepared the house for the closing—one of the hardest things I've ever done. Even writing this, years later, it still makes me tear up.

The buyer also tried to push me into a $10,000 reduction, based on a comment I wrote in an email, stating, "I will concede some of the costs not included in the contract." I told him I had a change of heart. If he still wanted the house, he needed to pay the contracted price, and he did. Honoring my boundaries paid off.

As you can see, everything I ask of you, working with me throughout this book, I have found to be true for myself. What I realized during the process of buying and selling my Notre Dame house was that, while I loved the house and its meaning, it created another burden for me that I didn't want or need. The closing came to its natural conclusion for the highest good of all concerned.

Today, former Notre Dame neighbors rent their home to me during football season. I pay about the same amount of money it previously cost me during that period, without any of the worries that go with owning out-of-state real estate. I just write a check, show up, and have a great time—all on my own terms.

## Setting and Holding Boundaries

Why is it so difficult to put ourselves first? Not doing so is detrimental to our financial health. Setting and respecting our personal boundaries is integral to our financial well-being. We all need to set healthy personal restrictions. I know we try, but then continually give in to others. It is not an easy lesson to learn, but when we do, the payoffs multiply positively through the years. Being "selfish" is a good thing. It means honoring yourself. It's the highest form of self-care and self-love and certainly the most self-nurturing.

I'll never understand why, particularly as women, we all too often put everyone else first. Men also tell me they get hung up on doing the "right" thing for others, ignoring their own needs. For example, a client named Tyler miscalculated his monetary needs for a six-month swing period between freelance jobs and was unsure where his $1,800 rent money was going to come from. He examined his investments and accounts and found a watch he could sell, valued at $1,800-$2,000, to cover his deficit.

At the same time the watch sale finalized, his son announced he was three months behind on his rent and needed $1,800. Tyler handed it over to him, never to be repaid, putting his son's needs over his own. Remember that, in most cases, the best way we can help someone is to hold our own boundaries and not bail them out, so they are able to learn the consequences of their own financial behaviors. This allows them to really see what they are creating and make different choices in the future. As well-meaning as Tyler was in the moment, his actions worked against both him and his son.

## Fears Live On

As my business grew, I noticed many people I worked with had lived through the Great Depression and feared being poor again. I was not too surprised those worries had not disappeared with that generation, despite how well many of them had done over the years.

Interestingly, that mentality continues to have an impact on many of us today—at times, including me. As I described earlier, I grew up only knowing a life of perpetual financial struggle, always living in survival mode, because someone in the family always needed something.

I remember, in college, I was making money to put myself through school. Then I would come home and see my sister needed a new pair of shoes. Her old pair was too tight, had holes in them, and her feet were growing. I carried student loan debt but used cash from my job to buy her new shoes. This put me over budget to meet my obligations and needs that month and took me into more debt.

## Walking, Talking Success

Healing myself and my clients led to the fine-tuning of PACT and eventually to success for people from all walks in life. What I am providing you with here is an entirely new way to look at and manage your financial affairs. I believe I have an antidote to what is ailing not only the industry today, but also the general public. My intention is nothing less than to shake up the entire financial services world by changing people's perspectives about money, allowing them to see money from the inside out.

The truth is, most people who enter my office say something similar to the following: "If I only had *more* money, all my problems would be solved"; "If I just made more, my life would be perfect"; or "What is everyone else doing—that I need to be doing—to have more money?" I will tell you what I tell them: "There are no *shoulds* when it comes to your money. You can create anything you choose." The PACT process explains *why*, in detail. Our emotional responses *create* our current financial status. Until we understand and process our buried emotions, we'll never achieve peaceful abundance—no matter how much money we make each year or how much we have in the bank.

## The Rich and Famous

It is pretty obvious, looking at the multitude of famous performers and athletes who make it big but then end up in debt and despair, that they amassed fortunes without understanding what to do with their wealth. On the opposite end of the spectrum, both of America's two wealthiest men, Bill Gates (net worth, as of this writing, $79.2B) and Warren Buffett (a distant second at a current $66.7B), created their own fortunes. Buffett, considered by many to be the greatest investor of all time, still lives in the modest home Omaha, Nebraska, that he bought in 1958 for $31,500.

Both men have committed to The Giving Pledge and dedicated the majority of their wealth to philanthropy. You might react by saying, "Yes, but they are very wealthy and can afford to give most of it away." Consider looking at it this way: they pursued what they loved and were wildly prosperous. It is truly philanthropic for them to give back to the country and the people who supported their success. Remember this, above all, from their success as self-made entrepreneurs: you are never too late or too young or too *anything* to stop dreaming and going after whatever you choose. Each and every one of us has the opportunity to determine the level of wealth we want. I am going to help you do just that.

## What Clients Most Want to Know

Whenever a client asks, "What can I be doing to improve my monetary situation?" PACT is my response. Clients are seeking something new, which is exactly what I offer you. There is that important first step: recognizing a point of reckoning and a call to action. This is where I make my announcement: "We are going to sit down and get financially naked!" After the initial shock, "Are you a crazy lady?" and the realization that we are keeping our clothes on, we get down to work, "disrobing" all of the secret unknowns they are experiencing around money, without consciously realizing how this is impacting their lives.

## It's a Process

We don't have to know how we are going to get where we want to be. The first step is visualizing ourselves already there. We have arrived! There are hints and whispers we receive from our higher selves, God, or the Universe. PACT helps clarify the details and lead the way.

Together, we get to work, unearthing the reality of where we are and then establishing the mini-steps and major goals to intelligently make tough financial choices, minimize student loan obligations, reduce or avoid debt, and achieve career goals. This might be the very first time you are considering a financial plan as the key to your entire life, one that truly offers you all the essential skills you need for living the life you choose.

## Flexibility and Willingness to Change

One of my employees had a tough time balancing her work and home life while her children were young. She was unable to do her job well because she was stretched too thin. With some creative scheduling, she was able to negotiate a four-day work week, arriving at ten o'clock each day. Initially, her salary and cash flow were impacted, but I helped her figure out her family budget. We shifted a few things around and, using some strategic budgeting, turned our problem into a win-win for her. Using PACT leads to creative and innovative solutions and infinite possibilities!

## We Are in This Together

Here we are now, you and I. You are ready to pursue your highest possible level of real wealth using PACT. I have a firm hold on your hand; together we are crossing over the threshold into a new personal financial freedom that will best serve your needs, dreams, and passions. I believe I should give you a quick overview of the PACT process before we dive into the details.

I will walk the walk with you, guiding you over every bridge. Together, we will identify and face long-standing assumptions, limiting beliefs, and shine light on your mental and emotional blocks; we'll then replace them with healthy, effective methodologies that will work for you throughout your lifetime.

PACT will teach you how to love your money. You won't mind opening your mail, paying your bills, and creating wealth by making your money work for you in ways that feed your soul. It's time for all of us to grow into financial independence with confidence, knowledge, and a sealed PACT with our money and our future.

# CHAPTER 3

# SIMPLY PACT

*What we really want to do is what we are really meant to do.*
*When we do what we are meant to do, money comes to us, doors*
*open for us, we feel useful, and the work we do feels like play.*
**~JULIA CAMERON**

The *Awaken Your Wealth's* PACT system provides you with a format to revamp your relationship with money, the feat I proudly accomplished in my own life and can now offer others. What I love most about PACT is that learning these simple techniques helps us appreciate and understand that real wealth is not only about money. *Real wealth* is truly a state of being, achieved not only by having what you want and need but by something even more critical: feeling rich in every facet of your life, financially, emotionally, and spiritually. Here you will learn practical steps to energize your financial resources so you feel rich in every way. You will learn a new approach towards your money and finances that will provide you with a phenomenal sense of relief and personal accomplishment.

PACT blends the heart and mind. As you will see, integrating the left-brain, logical financial approach with right-brain creativity and innovation enables you to pursue sustainable outcomes. You will live passionately, abundantly, and purposefully. We will combine traditional financial strategies with introspection and diverse energy modalities to once and for all reframe your personal relationship with money. As a result, your money will work *for you* to energize and support every facet of your life.

In this next section, each of the PACT concepts is briefly explained, along with the tools you will need to fully master the PACT process, which is then described in full detail in chapters 4, 5, 6, and 7.

---

*Who looks outside, dreams; who looks inside, awakes.*

~CARL JUNG

---

## PACT Begins with P: Picturing Yourself

The "P" in PACT literally means picturing yourself in the life your heart desires to be living. Do you remember what you wanted to be when you grew up? Does that have any relevance in your life today, or did you go in a totally different direction? One of the very first clients to use PACT demonstrated how powerful these four steps can be.

Peggy, age 55, always wanted to be a writer but worked as a nurse to pay the bills. Working with PACT, she learned to visualize herself writing, first as a medical professional, selling articles in her field, and then branching out into whatever her creativity might lead her to. After years of just talking about it, she actually became a working writer—within just 14 months—by blending her knowledge and experience in nursing with her heart's desire. She was amazed how these two worlds merged together.

Here are the tools you will need to use in chapter 4, "Picturing Yourself": a blank canvas, cork, or poster board; a journal; and the willingness to create time and space to meditate. These will help you map out your future for the life you will be manifesting. This is your chance to fulfill dreams you've always wanted and achieve goals for yourself and those you love. Think of the "your wish is my command" genie in Aladdin's lamp. In this story, you are the genie—fulfilling your own wishes.

## Using Visualization

Visualization is the ability to format visual images of abstract ideas or data mentally. This technique will help you reprogram your subconscious mind at the Alpha-Theta brain wave level, which is where the optimum value of visualization takes place. Researchers have shown that this brain frequency is the starting point for consciously creating and manifesting your reality. As you visualize a new way to see things, you will create *in your mind* exactly what you want to create *in your life*. It works in full circle. You will begin witnessing in your life what you've given life to in your mind. Can you see how that works? Some researchers recommend that you practice visualization for 20 minutes a day, while others say to do it at different times during your day. Whatever works for you is good and right. *Simply do it.*

Think about visualization as a way of mentally "rehearsing" the new reality you're creating, or you can view it as a better way to understand your world. Here are some examples:

- ♥ Are you tired of being in debt? This topic likely has many layers for you. It could be student loans, car debt, credit cards, mortgage, or parents or friends you owe money to.

Take the different debts and visualize each one in its own red-colored bucket. See the buckets begin to disappear, one by one. Watch how they drift away. Send them love and light for being there while you needed to lean on them to live the life you did at those moments. Now, I want you to see what's coming to you from the horizon. There are new, green-colored buckets, representing prosperity and growth. As they get closer, you notice each bucket has cash inside for your next car purchase, a college education fund, and money for your next shopping spree. What other green buckets do you have coming your way? These green buckets are funding for your desired lifestyle. You've said goodbye to having red buckets of debt and expressed gratitude for their prior purpose, but now you know those debts no longer serve you.

- ♥ Are you looking for a new relationship? See the person you imagine in every detail, with the qualities you are looking for. How do you feel when you are together? Express gratitude for that person now in your life, and he may come into your life sooner rather than later!

- ♥ Do you want to move into a new home? Visualize yourself in your dream house. Feel how comfortable you are with every lovely detail. Feel it in your heart and say thank you to the Universe.

- ♥ Maybe you desperately want to change jobs. Picture yourself in an ideal role for you, loving what you do, working the best number of hours you can imagine. Feel what it's like to get up in the morning to do this work, with the best type of co-workers, and what it feels like to be paid your ideal salary. Feel those bonuses as they hit your checking account. Express gratitude all around.

## Enjoy the View

This visualization will help you look at your life from a historical perspective, gaining wisdom and insight about the bigger picture. If someone can read this next exercise to you, great. Otherwise consider recording it so you can totally relax while working through the exercise.

Begin by closing your eyes and visualizing the story as it unfolds. As a newbie to this process, it might be easier to see the story with others in it first; then add yourself in and relate it to your own life. Begin by picturing the people who came before you and see how their experiences have shaped you. It's important to learn from history so we don't keep repeating it. Collectively, we can create a shift before reaching a crisis point. As President Abraham Lincoln so wisely put it, "Most folks are as happy as they choose to be."

## Visualizing Your Life

Close your eyes and calm your mind and body. Breathe gently and slowly as you listen to these words and create your own story about it. Allow yourself to feel the emotions that arise.

Visualize the family member in your life who lived through the Great Depression of the early 1930s. It could be a great-grandparent, grandparent, your own parents, or someone else who is important to you. Visualize pictures you've seen over the years of this period of time, when the Great Depression descended.

What family stories were you told or can you imagine happened? During the Depression, many people had to share their home with others, who were otherwise unable to survive. Do you know what line of work your forebears were in? How long were they out of work? What amenities, if any, did they have in life? There was very little paid work to go around at this time.

What do you imagine they valued most in their lives during this difficult time? Did they wonder where the next meal would come from? What did they live on? What were their fears? Imagine being so worried about what to feed your children or yourself that you can think of nothing else but the gnawing in your stomach. Feel the pain as a parent when you need to water down the milk to make it stretch. Feel the pain of worrying if your children are receiving the nourishment they need to stay healthy.

Many people survived the Depression by focusing on their life's purpose. They did what they needed to do. They learned to hone in on what was personally and financially most important, making tough decisions along the way.

Now think about how you felt in 2008 and 2009 when, financially speaking, the sky was falling in on our own economy. What did you fear? How was your job stability? Who did you know who lost his or her job, income, livelihood, or home? Did you sleep well during those tumultuous times?

What was important to you, and what became unimportant? Do you still have a bad feeling in the pit of your stomach when you think about all that uncertainty? How does this impact you today, or have you swept it all back under the rug?

Not everyone has fully processed the financial trauma experienced at that time. Minor steps have been made to financially heal our global economy. If you still have unresolved feelings, see yourself letting go and moving forward.

What could you do to live a more authentic life, with fewer worries about the ongoing upheaval that continues to rock you each day? Picture yourself coming to terms with your own unhealthy financial patterns. See yourself opening bills in envelopes covered with dust. See yourself paying off old debts that you've been dragging along with you far too long. Imagine the freedom of knowing your old habits are broken and healthy financial behaviors are now part of your daily routine. Watch yourself setting an example for others so that they, too, don't repeat years of poor financial choices.

Visualize the impact you are now having on your family and community, living in a healthy financial reality. Bask in the freedom of moneyed security. Express your joy and happiness. Envision what it would be like for everyone in the world to feel the same peace and security as you now do. See the whole world healthier and more financially stable, with everyone having what they need and living in peace with their decisions. Truly experience this in your heart space and let it fill every cell in your body. Sit with this peaceful feeling until you feel the urge to return to your place in the world.

---

*Authenticity starts in the heart.*
~**BRIAN D'ANGELO**

---

## The A in PACT: Accepting Reality and Awakening

After picturing yourself, it's time to learn how to accept your reality and awaken your authenticity by discovering your true intentions. We will break this step down into manageable categories (past, present, and future reality and intentions; and short-term, mid-term, and long-term reality and timelines) in order to continuously and consistently work toward clarity in each area as we move towards building your ideal life.

Self-acceptance means acknowledging who you are and what you've created up to this point—financially, professionally, personally, and spiritually. Authenticity means being real, open, and honest about who you are, what you want, and what you're here to do in this lifetime. Living as your authentic self is what fuels your success. Once your intentions are clear, the practical, hands-on skills you will be acquiring in chapters 6 and 7, "Choosing to Change" and

"Taking Action," will energize and fuel your life with the money and means necessary to confidently pursue your goals.

Coming up later, in chapter 5, "Accepting Your Reality and Awakening Your Authenticity," you will create the financial foundation needed to support what you want to achieve. There will be activities to help you identify the patterns in your life that have impacted your relationship to money up to this point.

Sean, age 25, became a client soon after his college graduation. Like his parents, he was so nervous about not having enough money to pay his bills that he refused to open any mail that appeared to be a bill. This was simultaneously occurring while he was considering changing jobs, since the first one he chose out of school was not in alignment with who he was on the inside, nor did he care for his boss in the least. He had no idea how to balance his online checking and savings accounts and used his credit and debit cards without keeping receipts. Looming also was serious student loan debt that would really impact his cash flow.

We began working with the basics, giving him the skills we should all learn in school, but don't, as I am sure you will agree. We'd be a lot more fiscally healthy if Money Management 101 was a required course for all high school students. Balancing a checkbook or online check register is a lost art, which really needs to be taught in middle school. Once Sean learned what he needed to know to manage his money from a new perspective, an inside-out perspective, he was amazed and delighted to realize he had enough to cover his expenses and could even put some money aside for savings, future vacations, emergencies, and even retirement.

Each and every one of us has within ourselves all we need to weather any ups and downs. On this journey, you become your own personal hero. When you uncover and embrace your authentic self, you will smile a lot more and feel much lighter.

*"We design our lives by the power of our choices."*
~RICHARD BACH

# The C in PACT: Choosing to Change

In order to consider the different choices you might like to be making, you need to begin by identifying those you have already made. The future is yours to design. What is it going to be? What positive financial selections will you make? What unhealthy financial decisions will you leave behind? What do you want to tackle first?

In chapter 6, "Choosing to Change," you will take what you learned by looking at and accepting your reality in the prior section and make a conscious choice to steer your life in another direction. By doing so, the person you were in the past must disappear completely to create the new you in the future. This doesn't happen overnight; it's a process over time. A variety of techniques will help you assess what brought you to where you are today and show you the new choices you can make to get where you want to go. As you will discover, it's quite invigorating to write out affirmations beginning with, "I choose to _____."

One of my very first clients, Gaby, widowed at age 38 with two young children, was quick to fill up an entire page with her priorities. She wrote the following vision: "I choose to figure out what I need to leave in savings in case I live to be 100 so that my children never have to worry about me. I also want to continue with the college funds my husband started and plan wonderful yearly vacations with my children, visiting places we would all like to see. We were supposed to go to Disney World last year, but my husband was ill, so that will be our first stop. Thank you, Julie, for helping me figure out my way forward."

> *The longer you're not taking action,*
> *the more money you're losing.*
> ~CARRIE WILKERSON

## PACT Ends with T: Taking Action

When it comes to money, we are most highly motivated to reach the finish line when clear and deliberate intentions are combined with taking action. Right now, at this very moment, you have the power to change your financial picture simply by turning your heart's desires and dreams into intentions. Many of my clients enjoy this "taking action" step the most because it applies to everything we do.

Lisa, age 45, was well educated and highly qualified for a variety of positions but afraid to change jobs. We reviewed the PACT stages, and she began picturing how she wanted to live: "I want to live in the city, in a downtown apartment, where I can meet more people and have more choices professionally. But I don't have the money to do that."

"What if we work together on how you can make that happen?" I asked. She looked simultaneously a bit doubtful and hopeful. Fortunately, it did not take her much time to take action, once she gave herself permission to consider the possibilities. She began applying for new jobs and looking for housing while she still worked at her old job and lived in the suburbs. Lisa had begun to believe that she could actually live the life of her dreams. Her action steps, exploring her options and valuing her worth, along with meditation and daily affirmations, helped her reach her goals. She did find a higher paying job in the city with a centrally located apartment right in the middle of a wide assortment of exciting activities and possibilities.

This step is expanded upon in chapter 7, the "Taking Action" chapter, which will walk you through a variety of enjoyable and enlightening exercises showing you how to prioritize your goals and take the steps needed. Your desires become the roadmap to accomplishing your new reality. There is also a built-in reward plan my clients love. It's important to reward yourself along the way for achievements accomplished, and surprise bonuses make it easier to follow through with your plans.

## Permission to Spend

Organizing your financials can be daunting, but it's critically important to have a realistic understanding of where things stand. It is also why you must find reasonable ways to reward yourself as you make your way through PACT. Building in rewards emotionally diffuses the tendency to act out frustrations financially. This one step of rewarding yourself can be instrumental in helping you stick to your plan and not give up. Go ahead and buy yourself something you would really enjoy having or go experience something you've always wanted to do.

Yes, you read that line correctly. Here I am, your financial planner, telling you to go blow through some money. Listen: when you follow your financial intentions while addressing your financial obligations, you deserve some financial fun in the process. This is all about having a wonderful time while creating your financially healthy and authentic self. Throw some of your reward money (that you earned by establishing a healthy relationship with your PACT plan and your cash flow) at activities and gifts you'll appreciate for a long time. Go for it!

Celebrating free things also brings joy. One of my best treats is to take my children out for a walk after dinner. Another is to do the grocery shopping all on my own, without children! And one of my super indulgences is to carve out the time to talk to a close childhood friend on the phone—something we rarely seem to get to do anymore. Sometimes we also just need to blow through a little of the hard-earned cash. Enjoy using it for something that will make you feel really good.

You deserve a prize along the way for reaching your goals. Have you been wanting to attend a concert or try a new restaurant? Would you like to go away for a weekend or buy a new pair of shoes? Scratch the itch by spending money on yourself, with cash earned, to pay for what you've wanted as a reward for healthy financial behavior.

As you work through PACT, small rewards may give way to larger ones. Perhaps you've been wanting a larger television but the one you have works just fine, and you can't justify spending the money. The next time you receive a chunk of cash, put about one-third of it into a named and designated savings account called "my reward bucket" or something like that. When the dollar amount reaches the cost of the big, beautiful new television of your dreams, buy it!

Just like my clients, you will get such a kick out of this self-reward system that you will keep thinking of bigger things you want to have or experience. Personal rewards are a real motivator to continue along your healthy financial path. Before you know it, you may very well be off enjoying your getaway vacation to recharge yourself physically, mentally, and spiritually.

*Whatever you believe with feeling becomes your reality.*
~**BRIAN TRACY**

## How Does It Feel?

It isn't how much money we have that impacts our spending and saving patterns. What's important are the intensely powerful thoughts and emotions about money that influence how we earn, save, and spend. Working through PACT encourages us to bring those feelings to the surface, reduce debts, and increase cash flow and savings. The good news is that once you understand the *impact* your emotions have on your financial behavior, you will learn to become an observer of your feelings by taking proactive steps. Once you begin using PACT, it all fits together and makes sense.

You absolutely can achieve the wealth and happiness you desire. The skills you will learn here will become more refined as you put them into practice. One of the most powerful ways to learn these lessons is through the exercises, personal assessments, and individual stories featured throughout this book.

MONEY ENERGIZING TIME:
## Tracking Your Economic Awareness and Behaviors

**ME TIME**

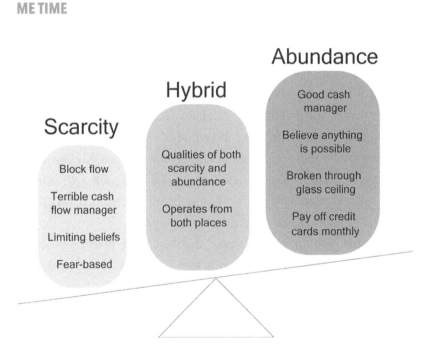

Figure 1: Economic Awareness Behaviors©

Using this sliding scale (see figure 1) will help you pinpoint your attitude towards money. This is all meant to help you understand where you fall on this spectrum and how to change areas that are not working at all or could be working more effectively. It might be very surprising to realize your feelings may range the gamut, from financial Scarcity to full financial Abundance. Let's look at the identifying characteristics of each of the three scenarios—Scarcity, Hybrid, and Abundance—to determine where you currently reside and the changes you need to make to create a different, more desired, financial future.

Considering this spectrum, what is your "money behavior"? Do you prefer to hand over your credit or debit card instead of using cash? Do you hear yourself saying, "I don't like using cash because I'll just spend it all at once, or it will burn a hole in my pocket?" Or do you convince yourself it's not safe to carry around cash in case it is lost or stolen? Behaviors like these indicate that money is your leaky faucet.

In this case, your financial energy would be considered low (labeled "Financial Scarcity" in figure 1), resulting in few promotions, below average job evaluations, and inadequate raises or bonuses. Unfortunately, when operating at this level, you become a magnet that attracts only those with similar energetic vibrations. Misery loves company. Spending time complaining about your job will attract people with similar grievances. Then none of you will get the raise, bonus, or promotion you want; like attracts like.

Chances also greatly increase that you will marry or select partners who also carry debt. This is true for all aspects of your life. As my mother—and perhaps yours, too—always said, "Two wrongs don't make a right." In essence, what you attract is a direct function of what you are sending out. Wherever you energetically resonate, which is whatever energetic vibration you put out, is what you will also bring in. In order to change what is happening to you and shift your outside world, you must improve your inner vibrational energy.

You know you are operating from a place of financial Scarcity when the income you have is never enough, you create lots of debt, and you just can't seem to get out of your own way. As human beings, we repeat the familiar. An important part of the PACT process is to recognize how you keep attracting what is familiar, often resulting in financial Scarcity. Every action has a reaction, so create a tactical game plan to shift out of those familiar roles.

Stop focusing on what you *don't* want and *don't* like. Think and talk about what you *do* want and *do* like. If you don't like your job, you are probably reinforcing it over and over by holding on to it out of fear. Are you thinking and even saying, "I hate my job, but I'm afraid to quit. Then what will I do?" Replace that negative energy vibration with a positive affirmation to lead you where you want to go: "I am ready to move on from this job to do what I love, at the income I expect, which I fully deserve. I release my current job to someone who will love having it, and I graciously accept this new great opportunity for myself." That sends a message to the Universe that you are ready to change.

## Stepping Up

The people in the center of this chart operate within the Hybrid Financial Model, being pulled between Scarcity and Abundance. When operating in Hybrid, you express both positive and negative, both high and low, energetic vibrations about your money at different times. While you might have a great cash flow, you find it's only a matter of time before resources slip through your fingers once again into Scarcity. Within the Hybrid Model, you live a financial life of polarities. Although you *know* how to attract money, you need to create a sustainable financial energetic vibration to keep you in the money. Another Hybrid characteristic is the fear that making a change will rock the boat. This is a sign of relinquishing your personal power by choosing not to handle your financial decisions and blaming others for your current situation.

If this is where you are on the spectrum, I will help you find your voice so you know that your opinions and feelings *do matter.* How do you find your voice? How do you release your initial response of blaming and judging others? PACT will help you acknowledge where you are not taking ownership of your financial life and provide the safe space to voice your opinion and desires and create concrete steps that will allow you to feel more empowered emotionally and financially.

On the far right of the spectrum is Abundance, characterized by having what you want and need and feeling fulfilled. Abundance is the ultimate goal and most wonderful place to be. It is also very important to recognize when we are living abundantly. Acknowledging your achievement and your desire to stay there by maintaining and growing more abundant is the key to self-fulfillment and financial success.

Many of us are somewhere in the middle of this spectrum, merging a bit of each side. We experience periods of Abundance but fall into Scarcity here and there. PACT is designed with the goal that we can become more permanently Abundant on all levels and live in a state of perpetual wealth.

---

*If you get the inside right, the outside will all fall into place.*
~**ECKHART TOLLE**

---

## Taking the Emotional Angst out of Investing

Emotions around money can create havoc for people trying to make intelligent investment choices. Angela, a 44-year-old divorced mother of three, came in for a consultation to review her retirement investment accounts (401k and IRAs) because she was changing jobs. Her portfolio totally surprised me. Here was this bright, highly successful woman who obviously used her feelings, rather than her intellect, when selecting investments. Angela was so afraid her children wouldn't have what they needed if something happened to her that she only purchased highly publicized insurance and annuity products to meet her savings and retirement needs.

She let her deepest fears rule and, in so doing, cheated herself. She traded the higher returns she could have been receiving for more expensive financial products and lower tax benefits because of her intense fear of losing money—which ironically was exactly what she *was* doing! As we talked, it became clear her fears stemmed directly from her childhood. In essence, Angela was repeating her parents' struggles. They were hard-working, middle class Americans who had good intentions to do the right thing financially, but during her childhood, the economy fluctuated dramatically.

She shared a family event imprinted upon her memory. Her father took a friend's advice to change jobs and walked away from a 10-year pension. Six months later, he was laid off. Unemployed for 14 months, her parents ran through their savings, and the family suffered on every level. The parallels to Angela's life were situations she created that decreased her savings for the future, repeating familiar familial patterns. The commonality is that as an adult, money slipped through her fingers as it had through her parents' grasp when she was a child.

When Angela was shown the actual monetary results of her emotional patterns, she was able to accept the reality of where she was and create a plan for exactly where she wanted to go. Sustainable healing comes from inside, whether it's restoring your body, your mind, your spirit, or your finances. We used PACT to shift her energy and to create a safety net to protect her children in case she suddenly died or could no longer work. Slowly we transferred her existing investments so they would put her money to work and match her goals, reinvesting half of the income back into the funds and the other half into rainy-day accounts.

Angela turned to meditation and affirmations to help break free of her fears from the past and make her own well-informed financial choices for the future. The bottom line of Angela's story is that wealth doesn't solely come from intelligently managing your money; prosperity comes from managing the *emotions* behind your money.

## The Overall ImPACT

PACT trains you to intentionally direct your money. If your money is not providing you with what you want in your life, you need to change the energy surrounding it. One of the main principles behind PACT is that whatever money you do have, you must use it purposefully to create your personal life design by prioritizing your intentions and setting goals.

When I decided to begin a journey to reach my desired weight, I joined a gym and religiously used the treadmill. Every session began with the same exact questions about my desired workout intensity, target heart rate, and weight. I consistently entered my ideal weight, not my actual weight. Day in and day out, I repeated the same routine. This eventually brought me to my desired weight. I changed my reality to what I *intended* it to be.

Believe me, I learned that the same exact thing can be done with money before I applied it to my weight. I actually use this technique for *everything*, including finding parking spaces on the busiest of downtown Chicago streets!

 MONEY ENERGIZING TIME:
## Quieting Your Mind

**ME TIME** Meditation works wonders for the mind, body, and soul and reinforces the power of setting intentions. No worries; it is very easy to learn. It is simply the action of quieting and relaxing the mind. You do not need to hire a guru to benefit from the practice.

If you have not meditated before and find it daunting, simply set aside five minutes in the morning when you first wake up to try it out. Some people find it easier to begin with guided meditation, accomplished by taking a class or listening to the recording of a soothing voice, with gentle music in the background, walking you through the process of breathing and calming yourself down. You'll be gently reminded to keep clearing your mind of any random thoughts or judgments. You can find many different types of guided meditations online if you wish to try that route. Personally, I love mantra meditation, which is when you repeat a specific word or phrase that causes you to energetically vibrate with what you want to attract.

Mantra meditations repeat a specific word or syllabic combination. One client uses the word "lovely" to focus on and repeat; another uses a vowel combination he finds soothing, "So-hum," and others prefer "Ah-men." Breathe in on the first syllable and breathe out on the second syllable.

Sit in a relaxed position in a chair, on the floor, or against pillows, whatever is most comfortable for you. Breathe in on the count of one through the nose; then breathe out through the nose, also counting one, slowly and comfortably. Then do the same for number two, in and out, then three, and so on. Simply focus on your breathing, in and out, slowly and deliberately, up to the count of 11, and then begin again.

As you do this, a variety of thoughts will cross your mind. Don't try to stop this from happening. Just let the thoughts come and go without putting your attention on them. Remain focused on your breathing. You can begin with only five minutes in the morning or evening and stretch it out slowly to about 20 minutes twice a day.

The true art of meditation is being mindful of your breath, slowing down your breathing, and quieting your mind. The words "meditation" and "mindfulness training" are often used interchangeably. For our purposes, use these guidelines to begin meditating and then tweak it to what works best for you and soothes your soul.

I feel the benefits of reduced stress and improved well-being almost immediately. The more you practice and do it each day, the better you will feel. Studies have reported significant changes in the brain and immune system from practicing just 20 minutes per day. Start practicing now so that you will be comfortable with it when we put these skills fully to work in PACT.

## All for One Means Better for All

Using PACT is similar to participating in community yoga or group meditation, where the work of everyone together results in multiple benefits for all. I know for sure that if everyone resolved their own financial issues, then many of the local, national, and global financial challenges would also begin to shift. Collectively, we have the power to move from a fear-based approach toward a much more collaborative environment, one in which individual creativity, innovation, and entrepreneurship rule the day. It all starts with you and me, learning a few new skills and increasing awareness of the possibilities to create our most-desired life. No matter where your money issues came from—growing up in poverty or affluence, being undervalued and underpaid, fearing wealth—together we can identify, modify, and change our money attitudes and our lives.

I saved my own financial future, along with helping thousands of others, with PACT. Together, we will walk the PACT path, opening every door we need to along the way. Join me now as we enter a healthier, happier, and more fulfilling relationship with financial independence. Let's begin to imPACT our lives and attain our own personal and financial independence. The Beatles sang "All You Need Is Love." True, love is definitely the core from which it all starts, but human beings also need safety, shelter, water, and food—all of which are supported by and dependent upon money.

## Finding What Works for You

What works for one person to shift energy blocks is different than what works for others, so you might want to try different natural healing modalities until you hit the one that works best for you. Once you start shifting your energy, you'll feel the freedom of shaking off negative patterns and blocks that no longer serve you. This will help you peel the layers away to uncover your authentic self.

Take a moment and picture energy frequency or vibrational levels on a scale from one to 10, one being low vibration and 10 being the highest vibration. We are constantly responding to our environment and experiences, moving at different times in and out of a variety of different vibrational levels. The lowest level is filled with negativity, criticism, blame, and victimization, which we must choose to leave behind, while the uppermost levels hold positivity, love, joy, acceptance, and success. I'm sure you've used the expressions, "I'm in a rut; nothing's going right," or, "I'm on a roll! This is great!" We have all experienced the opposite ends. Now it is up to us decide where we choose to reside. You are the driving force behind your energy shifts.

Consider the simple things you can do just about any time or place to raise your vibrational level and increase your energy flow, such as singing your heart out in the car, going for a run in the park, or watching a really funny movie and laughing out loud. Years ago, I attended a women's group where the leader instructed us to sing and dance along to the Diana Ross song "I'm Coming Out." She said it would help us shake out our old energy to create space for new possibilities.

Holy Cow, that was way out of my comfort zone, but she was totally right. It worked! My higher energetic vibration left me buzzing. It's so simple, and you can do it anywhere. Now I sing and dance with my kids at home, playing different music they love, whenever we need to shake things up and feel better. It's simple but effective. And I will publicly admit that I have moved on from singing Diana Ross to singing "Let It Go!" from the movie *Frozen*.

## Try Something New for You

There are literally thousands of energy-healing therapies available. I suggest different ones to my clients all the time. Healers come from a wide variety of backgrounds and bring to their work natural gifts and specialized training. There are many free resources online you can check out on your own to shift personal energy and overcome both exterior and interior blocks. Some of you are probably already familiar with the power and benefits of holistic practices and therapies, while others are wondering about their validity. Holistic healing is a brand new, totally unknown concept to many of you, especially when applied to financial planning.

## Deliberate Finger Tapping

I often recommend yoga, meditation, tai chi, hypnotherapy, energy healers, Holographic Re-patterning, and acupuncture. Why would a financial planner refer clients to these types of esoteric, strategic alliances? It might seem a bit foreign, but this is an integral piece of the PACT equation. There is absolutely no way you can actually shift yourself financially if you don't shift your personal energetic vibration. This is worth repeating: to achieve abundance and prosperity, you must shift your personal energetic frequency. While we are planning tactical financial steps, we need to have you energetically align from the inside out. This is what creates a sustainable reality for the life you desire.

Nick Ortner is the CEO of The Tapping Solution and author of *The Tapping Solution: A Revolutionary System for Stress-Free Living*. Tapping first achieved success on the Internet with YouTube videos that enabled viewers to immediately tap out tension and blocked pressure points. Ortner combines Chinese acupressure and psychology to improve health, well-being, wealth, relationships, and more. I found it most effective for releasing negative feelings and beliefs while opening myself up to acceptance and abundance. It's also great for dissipating chronic headaches, along with neck and shoulder pains.

Holographic Re-patterning®, also referred to as Resonance Repatterning®, is built upon research and findings that there is an optimal frequency range for physical, emotional, and mental health. Practitioners offer sessions that use muscle testing (applied kinesiology) to identify problem areas. This technique, too, has abundant, free information online. The emphasis is on self-healing and enabling followers to create positive changes, including identifying unconscious, repetitive, and ingrained behavior patterns and energy blocks.

Open yourself up to the possibilities. There are a wide variety of modalities and techniques you can use to shift the energy in your life. The PACT process reflects, expands, and shifts your body's energies. Many of my clients turn to holistic practices to move things quickly along and break down barriers that have held their bodies and minds hostage for years. Often, as was the case in this next story, the key is consistent and determined actions and intentions that move you forward.

## MICHAEL AND MAGGIE:
# Seeking and Finding Their Next Steps

Old friends and new clients, Michael and Maggie had been happily living in San Francisco, California, when they decided to move back home to Boston, Massachusetts, to raise their daughter around their extended family, similar to the way they grew up with grandparents and cousins all around. After settling in, they realized they needed to rethink their careers and face the question, "Now what?" Unable to secure ideal work in their former fields of accounting and running a speaker's bureau, they felt disoriented and unsure of their future, which put pressure on their marriage. The downside was receiving nonstop, unsolicited advice from family members, but the upside was the opportunity to start over with a clean slate, moving in a new direction.

Friends set them up with jobs in the Boston suburbs that brought in the requisite cash flow to support their family. Michael was very clear that his new job would be okay in the interim, but kept seeking clarity on what he really wanted for his career. He considered working with small businesses, being a financial planner, and starting his own company, but he had no clue as to how to put it all together. He just kept talking about what he wanted and continued working with Maggie on their personal, work, family, and financial intentions. He also took a lot of flak from well-meaning relatives because he turned down a few job offers with six figure incomes that he believed would negatively impact their quality of life. He was certain that he did not want to return to the rat race, but at the same time, he felt pressured to make the wise, acceptable, and expected decision to take what others saw as great job offers.

Another friend kept begging him, "Please, you've got to meet my friends. You guys are the perfect match." Finally, he gave in and said, "Sure." During that meeting, everything fell into place. It was a small company looking to hire a financial planner they could groom to buy the business from them when they retired. Michael and Maggie were thrilled because it was everything he'd been looking for all along. Sometimes we just need to hold on to our intentions and allow the Universe to line it up for us. Then it all shows up better than we ever could have imagined. The key is to pay attention when it does.

## Assessing Your Money Energy Level

Sometimes all you need to assess your energy level around money is to call upon your innate body intelligence. Our bodies are just as clever as our minds. When we pay attention, our physicality tells us now what is good for us and what is not so great. Have you ever felt anxious any time a certain topic around money or work comes up? That anxiety is your "gut feeling"; it's your body talking. Or maybe you turn defensive when your partner wants to discuss the family budget. You might open up your bills when they arrive, or you may deliberately choose to make a big pile in a corner. These are ways of avoiding what we fear or don't understand.

Do yourself a favor. Pay attention to your emotional reactions around money, career, earnings, and savings. Do you bite your fingernails or turn into a mass of quivering jelly at the mere mention of money? Instead, become an objective observer. Make notes to identify your own personal patterns. Once you are aware of your feelings and reactions, particularly the ones that are no longer working for you, seek solutions, as Michael and Maggie did, by working through the layers.

I know what it is like because I have been the seeker, and now I am the sought-after, which is quite enjoyable and magical. I love it when people find me through social media, books, workshops, or client referrals. When we first meet, new clients often appear a bit lost and talk about feeling like something's missing in their financial lives, but can't quite figure it out. When I explain what I do, it's the breath of fresh air that provides the space they need to create an original path for themselves. I become the guide for their new money

PACT, providing a safe place to shift, heal, make new choices, see themselves realistically, and move bravely ahead.

## Rarely a Straight Line

Most of us began our careers in our mid-20s with great and wonderful expectations but found that career path was not quite right at age 35, 45, 55, or beyond. You may need to change jobs, try a new career, or work fewer hours, but you're afraid to rock the boat. You have evolved, but perhaps your job or your co-workers have not. Once you are conscious of your new reality, you can never go back and "sit on the same barstool." Not only is that a great metaphor for someone Irish like myself, but it also captures the changes we experience in our lives.

If you have stayed in a toxic work environment for too long, you're probably full of negative self-talk and you may feel defeated. You hate the job, but you can't afford to leave. You are not thriving any longer because you have lost the key components to feeling whole and successful. PACT gives you the tools to regain your life's dreams, meaning, and purpose. Your compelling reasons to change will shift your internal energy, enabling you to make your next move.

## CHRIS AND JENNY:
## Changing Career Energy

I don't have to look far for dramatic examples of transformation since they walk into my office every day. Chris and Jenny, in their mid-30s, seemed anxious from the moment they began talking. Jenny had worked at her current job with a large national company for 13 years. She wanted to make a change because it was no longer fulfilling, but with a second baby on the way, she was afraid to take the risk. She felt stuck and believed she had no open options. In addition, they hated where they lived and wanted to raise their family somewhere warmer and closer to nature.

Sensing they were at a major crossroads, I wanted our discussion and financial solutions to match their needs and wants. I asked Jenny, "If being married and having a baby on the way was not your current reality, what would you want to be doing? What are you really passionate about in your work life?" She said she didn't know—which meant she really was stuck because she lacked a compelling reason to change.

I encouraged her to shift her thinking and become an observer of her career, looking at it from the outside so she could tell me what she *felt*. She was most uncomfortable thinking about her job and kept repeating, "I don't know." I broke it down into smaller pieces and asked if she resonated with the current management of her division. "No, absolutely not," she quickly responded. Clearly she had an opinion, but was so paralyzed and overwhelmed she couldn't imagine what she wanted. I asked if there was any part of her job that she loved. Not surprisingly, she responded with what she *hated*—bringing in sales. All of her 13 years' experience was in retail sales.

Then I asked, "What is it that you do like about your current job? Or what could you see yourself doing?" She could see herself taking over the management of retail sales because then she could use what she knew from experience and could teach others from a managerial position. Hurray, there was the bridge from her old world to the new one! The major challenge was that she didn't know how to get there. I urged her to detach from the outcome and stay in brainstorming mode to uncover her compelling reason to move.

Then I asked one more question: "Are there retail management opportunities somewhere else in the country where you might like to go?" Yes, it turned out that she resonated with the national vice-president of sales' vision and could see herself working with the company's Southern California team. Jenny had just revealed the possibility that her job path could take them both to Southern California with the same company. They were thrilled by the thought of leaving the Midwest for a warmer climate, without a huge risk. And there it was—the remainder of the compelling reason.

I did the same thing with Chris, with similar results. They had both articulated where they wanted to live and the transition to their desired jobs. They left my office with the beginning of a financial plan and began planting the seeds for their move. Interestingly, management suddenly shifted, and the position Jenny wanted opened up—but where they currently lived. This actually gave them time to have their second child and allowed her to build a resume towards the new job to justify a transfer with a 30 percent pay hike. It was the perfect example of how things show up when you find your catalyst for change and claim what you want. Jenny and Chris were far more open to the infinite possibilities than they initially realized!

## Energy in Motion

The PACT process uses emotional energy, human heart energy, to help you see and move beyond self-limiting beliefs. It was only when Jenny observed herself from outside her body, without overanalyzing the situation in her head, that she was able to move forward. PACT is designed to help you dream big in all areas of your life, revealing the choices and action steps to make it happen for real.

**ME TIME**

MONEY ENERGIZING TIME:
## Getting in Touch with Your Money Emotions

Now we have discussed a few examples, it's time for you to get in touch with some of your own feelings. Keep one notebook designated just for these exercises and for journaling as you work your way through the book. While reading Chris and Jenny's story, what came up for you? Give yourself time to respond to every question. Do not edit yourself—simply write out responses as they appear.

## Money Matters

- ♥ When thinking about money, what are your most immediate thoughts?
- ♥ How do you feel?
- ♥ Do certain words or money responsibilities give you a queasy feeling in the pit of your stomach?
- ♥ Do you get excited or energized by your financial picture?
- ♥ Is there something missing in your money photo?
- ♥ Do you long for or seek something else?

Can you describe what you are looking for? Record as many thoughts as you can as your emotions pour out. Be honest with yourself. Think about where your particular beliefs, fears, or anxieties might have originated. Can you describe how your parents handled and responded to money? Are you repeating their old patterns, or did you choose to go completely opposite of their approach to avoid what they did? Remember, these answers are not good or bad. They simply are.

## BRENDA AND EDDIE:
# Finding Financial Collaboration

A newlywed couple in their late 20s, Brenda and Eddie found themselves on their fifth wedding anniversary on opposite sides of their housing issue. When they were first married, they lived in university housing as they both worked on graduate degrees. They assumed they would move together wherever they found work but never discussed their differing views on homes and mortgages. Brenda grew up with a mother who cried for months over buying the family's first home. She was overcome by the responsibility of the mortgage and the permanency of the decision. Subconsciously, Brenda imprinted her mother's experience and only wanted to rent, whereas Eddie's extended family was in real estate, specializing in buying prime properties in desirable locations, making improvements, and quickly turning them over. He grew up believing renting meant throwing money out the window.

## What Do You Believe?

Our beliefs about money and negotiating come from observing what happens all around us. Our view of love comes from our relationships with our mothers, and our belief about worthiness comes from our fathers. Researchers have shown how whole you feel as an adult is directly dependent upon how safe you felt growing up.

Consider each of these four core beliefs: love, self-worth, wholeness, and safety. Write down the adjectives and words that describe your core beliefs. Examine what they are and where they came from. Ask yourself if you still want the old emotions and possibly limiting beliefs to be driving your life. If you polled 10 strangers and asked them to do this same exercise, you'd probably find similar concerns to your own. We all have past programming that grows with us into adulthood. It's our job to make sure our current beliefs are true, applicable, and working for us, rather than against us.

As you proceed through PACT in the upcoming chapters, you will find a multitude of ways to work through old thinking and feeling patterns. Once you clean out the old to make room for the new, you will be free to create the life you choose. An important first step is to begin turning any negative thinking positive.

## Excuse Me, What Did You Just Say?

How do you talk to yourself? When analyzing investment opportunities, what is your message to yourself? Do you ask yourself, *Are you about to make another stupid decision?* Or, do you affirm your power: *I choose to research this a bit more before making a decision?* Would you be embarrassed if someone else heard your self-talk? Those private little conversations you have with yourself are the dialogue or chatter that plays out in your mind. It is very important to practice positive self-talk by replacing negative, demeaning thoughts with empowering and inspiring words and actions.

The solution starts with you. Pay attention to your self-talk, particularly around money and finances. Do these topics bring out the best in you? *What a great move you just made, changing to a higher interest account. I'm proud of you.* Or do they keep you in a vicious cycle of struggle or repeating the familiar, such as, *Where was your brain, leaving that money earning so little for so long? Will you ever learn?*

When you catch yourself using vocabulary that seems to be more reactive and alarming than productive, reframe it, as I've done in the examples above and below. The goal is to internalize a positive approach to your thinking and speaking. Say these out loud. Select two or three to repeat during your day. Write them out. Say them to yourself in the mirror. Whenever you hear yourself being negative, stop! Deliberately replace negative messages with positive affirmations to shift even the most deeply rooted, destructive beliefs and improve your self-image and self-confidence.

- ♥ *I never have enough money for what I need.* Replace with, "The Universe provides me with all of the money I will ever need."
- ♥ *No matter what I do, I can't get out of debt.* Replace with, "I am making responsible decisions for my money. I am pleased and proud of my relationship with money."

- ♥ *See, I told you so. You're not so smart after all.* Replace with, "I learn and grow from every experience. I am proud of who I am. I love me!"
- ♥ *Why can't I be wealthy and do what I love?* Replace with, "I am wealthy in every aspect of my life. I love what I do. It fuels and nurtures me and supplies me with all I need to successfully live and enjoy my life."
- ♥ *How am I going to live the lifestyle I want and still pay the bills?* Replace with, "I support myself, and the Universe supports me. I love what I do and give thanks that my work provides me with everything I need to support my lifestyle."
- ♥ *How do I transition from my current reality to my desired life?* Replace with, "I am true to myself in everything I do. I fully understand my current reality and how it leads me, step-by-step, into my desired lifestyle."

## Making the Best of Your Feminine and Masculine Energy

Born male or female, we have both feminine and masculine energies at our core. These attributes help us figure out how things work. We strategize our inner world with our feminine side and decipher the outer world with the masculine side, and both should work in concert with each other. When in a business situation, my masculine energy flares up. At home, I'm a nurturing mom full of feminine energy and can call upon either side of me as needed. PACT enables us to assess, balance, and integrate our lives, using these powerful energies to our advantage.

Men and women tend to view and handle their money matters differently. Sometimes it's the woman who likes to plan every detail and finds comfort in a predictable outcome, while the husband might prefer spending now and adding things up later. Of course, it could also be the opposite. I've met couples where both enjoy handling multiple financial situations together as a team. However, the majority of male clients I have worked with possess a singular focus or goal, unwilling to waiver until it is accomplished or before moving on to the next challenge.

Sometimes that's great, and at other times, it's important to remember there is more than one way to achieve positive end results. Internal feminine energy is often called "being" energy—the ability to just sit, think, and be creative, collaborative, and innovative. Nurturing traits emanate from the inner feminine appreciation for beauty and nature. Using intuition and gut feelings to make decisions are skills used by both sexes. The feminine side enables receptivity to all the good offered to you so that you can receive protection and guidance from the Universe.

## PACT Works Your Feminine and Masculine Energies

PACT calls upon and uses your feminine energies, particularly as we work through chapter 4, "Picturing Yourself," and chapter 5, "Accepting Your Reality and Awakening Your Authenticity." The focus in these chapters is on *being, feeling,* and *thinking* about your situation. These initial steps are critical as you seek sustainable financial success but are too often ignored by mainstream financial professionals.

Reviewing Chris and Jenny's story demonstrates how profound it can be to acknowledge and activate your internal authority and desires. Jenny tapped into her feminine energy when she began dreaming about her options, thinking deeply about her job and observing what she was living. She felt the emotions of her dreams and aspirations, as well as her anger, sadness, and frustration with her job. This created an emotional space that allowed her to see the opportunities for change that were open to her. Then she tapped into her inner masculine energy, which helped her take action, receive a

30 percent raise, and move with her husband and children to a more desirable living and working solution for them all.

## Tapping into Your Inner Masculine Energy

Masculine energy helps with practical, day-to-day financial responsibilities. This side is rational, tactical, logical, and analytical. These areas may not be your strengths; however, you do have access to them. If you don't feel very logical or analytical, that could be because you do not tend to use these skills much. Think of it like yoga, where each position is practiced on each side of the body to create balance. We need to do the same thing here. Masculine energy is the "doing" part of your inner self.

One of my closest friends tells a story about the day she walked out of the train station with her daughter. Shots were fired somewhere nearby, and she slammed her 10-year-old daughter against the wall and shielded her tightly with her body. Her feminine energy rose to protect her child, first and foremost, and her masculine energy flew into action. Other male energies include competitiveness, presence, manual labor, leadership, and achievement. I know I can see a tremendous overlap in myself and my children with all of these traits.

The PACT activities and exercises in chapter 6, "Choosing to Change," and chapter 7, "Taking Action," will show you how to access your inner masculine energies. We use our inner feminine energy to process and feel our emotions around money matters. For practical and logical daily financial decisions, we use our inner masculine energy. This yin-yang energy serves to balance and complete us in many situations and relationships.

## JULIE'S GEMS:
## Balancing Household Roles

Joe and Stacy, while accessing their internal energies, have found a good working balance. Nurturing comes naturally to Joe and was instrumental in his decision to teach and coach. With four young children, he is now their CHO, chief household officer, otherwise known as a stay-at-home Dad. He takes the lead in tending to the children's needs, while Stacy is a very happy entrepreneur running her own company and financially supporting them.

They each choose to exercise specific internal energies, depending upon the need and circumstance. Both masculine and feminine energies are needed to balance and sustain families, partnerships, businesses, and finances. By recognizing and tapping into the power and purpose of each and every available energy, you can work towards financial restoration and growth.

## Shifting Attitudes and Emotions

Couples enter my office with varying degrees of feminine and masculine focus. They may agree wholeheartedly with my financial process, or not, depending on how they see the world. One couple who started off denying their economic turmoil learned to identify the sources of their denial and appreciate the value of the financial healing process as they worked their way through the PACT process.

Jessica and Peter came in as a couple, but she kept asking to speak with me privately—so she could coach me on how to best handle her husband. "Julie, I understand what you're getting at when you say we should be feeding our hearts and honoring where we're at emotionally, but when we come in next time and you speak to

Peter, could you please just stick to the numbers?" she pleaded and apologized in the same breath. "Otherwise, he won't value your level of expertise."

Jessica understood that Peter was in denial about his decreasing salary and need to change jobs. What she did not realize is that he was in denial over his emotional relationship with money. Perhaps he would have said the same thing about his wife: "She is the one who just can't face the financial truth." My job is to help everyone involved remove the rose-colored glasses so he or she can see and understand what is really going on. It is not unusual for two contributing members in a relationship to vibe on different wave lengths. Perhaps you can see yourself in this scenario. If so, you're in the right place to create your solution.

Peter and Jessica were both commissioned salespeople, working for different companies and used to bringing in hefty incomes, but their assets kept slipping away. What brought them to me was that Peter's business income had rapidly decreased. He was unable to acknowledge that he needed to make a major shift in his work life. I totally appreciated and understood Jessica's concern for his emotional struggle. Clearly he was stuck between his loyalty to a company he had helped grow and the realization that it was time to go. My job was to help them avert a disaster.

We ran their numbers, explaining how competitive each investment was compared to the indexes, knowing that wasn't the real issue. But Jessica was right; Peter liked numbers and believed them. That piece of information helped me make a plan. In cases like Jessica and Peter's, the key is to establish a safe space for the more left-brain, logical-minded person. My recommendation to Jessica was, "Let him be where he is and allow him to come to a realization on his own time, without pushing or judging. Using force will only cause massive combustion and deterioration, rather than improvement."

We worked our way through PACT together. I waited until our third meeting to share a five-year comparison chart I created, showing him the decline in his income. He stared at it. I'm sure there wasn't anything on that piece of paper he did not already know, but it was his moment of reckoning. "It looks like it's time to jump off a sinking ship," he whispered. "Guess I need to find a new source of income."

Sometimes the reality is that we can't imagine doing something differently—which is where Peter was stuck. He loved his job and the people he worked with so much that he believed he couldn't handle leaving them. But their business had run its course. Before leaving my office, Jessica and Peter made calls to friends and contacts to let them know Peter was willing to consider a few different fields, as long as he could stay in commissioned sales.

## Accepting When the Time Is Right

I have seen this first-hand in my own relationships and know how it works. I would tell one of my ex's something I think he should consider: "You need to keep up with your exercising every day to maintain your health," or, "I'd really like you to have your own savings account on the side, to treat yourself with something you'd really like to have or to experience something just for you." He ignored me, but then he would hear the same exact words from one of his friends or a male motivational speaker, and he would have a light bulb moment, as if it is the very first time he heard such a brilliant idea.

Initially, I was frustrated because I knew I had told him the same exact thing. Then I realized we all hear messages in our own divine time. My job is to respect his right to take the knowledge he gained in his own way and let it move him to the next path in his journey in his own time.

I, too, need and want others to hold such a safe space open for me. It does not matter that he heard the same message more clearly from someone else. I'm grateful he received it. Too often we try pushing those closest to us to hear us. We just need to let it go. It's not in our timing; it's in theirs. The more we push, the more miserable we all become. Who needs that?

## Winning the Lottery

Throughout the years, I have had several clients win the lottery. Let's put this in perspective. One day you're earning a paycheck, and the next you have a windfall of hundreds of millions of dollars. Suddenly, long-lost family members, friends, and strangers appear, begging the lucky winner to pay down their debts and give them a fresh start. The message here is that money does not solve everything. Truth be told, neither the lottery winners themselves nor the family members or friends receiving bailouts actually achieve the "fresh, clean slate" they sought. In each and every case, the clean slate theory did not work.

Within three to five years, these lottery winners were back to their original financial set point because they never resolved their core issues, fears, and subconscious beliefs about how money works and their relationship to it. This "clean slate" mentality is commonly found when inheriting money, declaring bankruptcy, receiving a bonus at work, or tax return in April. The only way to achieve financial healing is to clean up a financial mess. Allow yourself to feel the emotional pain of the past and create the infrastructure to respond to a future filled with financial Abundance.

## Let's Go PACT!

Congratulations. We have reached the point where we are certainly ready to put your financial life in order through the PACT process—built from your core, your soul, your very being. It's easy and practical. Tackle it one step at a time and follow the introspection and action steps, which will lead you to true financial healing.

There are only a few more techniques I want to share to help you shift your energy from your current financial position to a more abundant one. No longer will you fall prey to those quick fixes that promise you the world but in the long run simply don't work. PACT is a *proven* and *workable* solution. Love yourself enough and find the courage to proceed. We are almost there.

---

*You can do the seemingly impossible. All you have to do is break it down into possible steps.*
~KEVIN MCGOVERN

---

## Additional Tools and Skills You'll Be Using in PACT: Muscle Building

Dealing with and building a positive outlook about your financial reality is very much like building up your muscles. If you don't use it, you lose it. Regular trips to the gym are required to build your body's muscles; consistent exercising is also needed to build up your *financial* muscle strength. No matter how much you work out, you won't hit your fitness goals if you're not fed the appropriate nourishment along the way. Similarly, financial muscles need the PACT process formula of big, beautiful, limitless dreaming. In chapter 4, you'll learn how to dream big to fuel your goals.

Once you begin, keep practicing what you're learning, or the same old scenarios will keep repeating. I will show you how to exercise your financial muscles and improve your relationship with your money. Building up your financial strength begins with choosing to put you and your dreams first. Don't get sidetracked by trying to figure out all the actions you need to take. Just aim to clearly identify what you want and dream of accomplishing. This is the essential first step: we claim our authentic selves and determine what we want, and then we create the opportunity for it to come to us.

## Doing Your Exercises for Life

In order to build this muscle, you need to pick the most appropriate type of exercise to start with, just as you would at a health club. Do you want to lift weights, stretch with yoga, or do cardio? Once you pick cardio, which machine do you want: the bike, elliptical machine, or treadmill? Your life works the same way. Your financial life is driven by the decisions you make in other areas of your life: work, family, and personal life. Decide which area you choose to build up and design first.

You'll be using a series of exercises to drill down and specify your intentions. As you build your confidence by setting your intentions and begin witnessing the desired results, you will move up to the next level, just as you would on a treadmill. If you start at three miles per hour, you can continually progress to higher speeds. Simply accept your individual starting point and allow yourself to build your financial muscle at a steady pace over time. This is not a race. Just start growing from where you are planted, and together we will walk the walk.

## How *Do* the Rich Get Richer?

When you are clear in your intentions, it's electrifying and transformational. Being excited about life actually causes you to operate at a higher vibrational level. This is what I call your "pull-in" energy. When you are clear about what you want, claim it, and back it up by your daily behaviors. Your pull-in energy acts like a magnet, bringing you everything and anything you've ever wanted. This is a major reason why the rich get richer.

Unfortunately, if you are struggling financially, you tend to feel miserable and defeated. There's nothing to be excited about. People without much money say they feel like they're being taken advantage of. In reality, they are being defeated by their own self-talk and behaviors. If they just keep talking about how badly they are being treated, they keep creating situations where money can't come to them. They're energetically blocking it. Why? Because they are resonating and vibrating with *financial Scarcity.*

The Universe gives you what you ask for, not only through your words but also via your energetic vibration. If someone says, "Don't think of a pink elephant," you can only see the unwanted pink elephant. It works the same way with the words and feelings you put out into the world. If you keep thinking you're going to lose your job and function within a paralyzing state of fear, why are you surprised when you get laid off? You brought it on. The moral of the story is this: watch your language. Keep your words, thoughts, and feelings positive rather than negative because miracles are waiting to happen for you.

Speaking of which, your miracles are however you define them. Real wealth is not about a specific dollar amount or achievement, but rather it means living abundantly in all areas of your life—family, personal, career, financial, and spiritual—from your heart space, as you will see in the insert below.

## Living a Heart-Centered Life

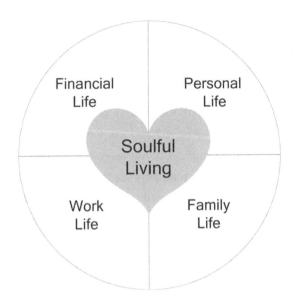

Figure 2: Living a Heart-Centered Life

## Living Life on Your Own Terms

Deborah is one of the most authentic and wealthy people I know. She embodies what it means to live a soulful, heart-centered life, choosing to be her own authority, guide, and decision-maker. Widowed in her 30s, she raised her children on her own. She worked at a company she loved and retired when she chose to—in her early 60s.

Here's the key: when she was working, she did not live on her entire annual salary of $70K. She maxed out her 401k annually, paid off her house early, and never had credit card revolving debt. She lived comfortably below her means, rather than beyond them. All of these elements created financial space and provided her with real choices. She has always kept at least six months of her living expenses in a separate savings account and still does. Her Social Security is about

$1,600 per month, with her investments paying out about $900 per month to meet her $2,500 monthly expenses.

She considers the equity in her home as "saved" money for LTC (long term care) if it is ever needed. Within months of leaving her full-time job, she began working part-time in a local bakery because it was fun. She loves the baking, selling, and the social scene. Deborah lives abundantly for Deborah. While others might choose to travel or relax at home, she loves her life because it's simple, easy, and makes her tick. She laughs all the time and has no regrets. When her children experience a crisis or drama in their lives, she's supportive without taking it on. Her boundaries are healthy and clear, adding comfort, peace, and years to her life. "I tell my grown children and grandkids that the greatest gift I can give them is taking good care of myself so I will not be a burden to anyone else," says Deborah.

I'm proud of Deborah because she created her own life on her own terms. She has a wealth of purpose and passion that we can all learn from. It's all in how you choose to define what you want it to be; then live it.

## Different Strokes for Different Folks

Every person's story is different. I would feel restricted living on $2,500 a month because my self-definition is to travel the world with my family, donate to causes I believe in, and help others by being an angel investor. But that's my self-definition. You are the artist of your life. We all have a blank canvas to fill with our heart's desires. Create the masterpiece you choose to live. Be the star of your own story.

## THE ImPACTful Skills You Need to Know

Just before we move into the PACT process, here are a few more specific skills and practices that will greatly facilitate your financial and personal transformation. These preliminary exercises will strengthen your internal "muscles" to create a powerful internal space for the forthcoming PACT process. By developing these skills, you are laying the foundation for your journey through PACT.

I've mentioned affirmations earlier in the book, and we've used them to help shift our energy. Now we'll consider and practice additional affirmations and follow up with using meditation, intuition, and visualization. If you already know and practice these techniques daily, excellent! Sort through these to see which you can add to your practice. If these concepts are new to you, practicing these skills will help you prepare to fully understand and use the PACT process, with your "muscles" in optimum shape. Here's what you most need to know to use PACT.

## The Power of Affirmations

The origin of the word affirmation is from Latin: *to strengthen.* I am convinced that affirmations strengthen your ability to create your own story and have your life unfold the way you choose. W*e are what we think and feel.* Our daily actions grow out of our thoughts and feelings, and affirmations are comprised of positive and intentional ones. They are the reinforcements needed to stay on track. Studies have shown that repeating affirmations out loud, or saying them silently with frequency and passion, can restructure your mind, body, and spirit. Writing them down over and over also brings about the positive reinforcement of every phrase.

I select three affirmations at a time to work on, internalizing them, not only as part of my daily thoughts, but also my feeling patterns. Everywhere I look, I see them written on Post-It Notes decorating my fridge, laptop, bathroom, bedroom mirrors, and car. Saying them while looking at yourself in a mirror is a very powerful way to increase the staying power of the changes you are making. Keep reciting them over and over. Often after a long day of running a company and dealing with four children, I mumble them off as I fall asleep at night and then again in the morning. Do what works for you.

Readers of my first book, *The Emotion Behind Money: Building Wealth from the Inside Out,* shared that the affirmations led to many positive results. I'm happy to include new ones with a financial component here for you. Earlier in this book, we discussed "I choose" affirmations. These are built upon the "I am" statement format. Please notice that these do not include wishing or hoping words. It is far more powerful to say affirmations as if the words are already true in your life. Allow them to spark your heart to "feel" your new reality. For psychological and emotional reasons, affirmations are in the present tense and use positive language that personally relates to you. Using the words "I am" puts you exactly where you want to be.

---

*We are what we think.*
*All that we are arises with our thoughts.*
*With our thoughts, we make the world.*
*~*THE BUDDHA SIDDHARTHA GAUTAMA

---

## MONEY ENERGIZING TIME:
## Practicing Affirmations

**ME TIME**   Use these affirmations as you work through the PACT process:

- ♥ I am financially independent.
- ♥ I am worthy of receiving all good things.
- ♥ I am who I want to be and where I want to be.

- ❤ I am happy for you and all that you have. I am part of this abundant world where there is plenty for everyone, including me.
- ❤ I am a money magnet.

These affirmations help you create your own new reality. The words do not have to be absolutely true for you in this moment. You are imprinting on your brain the way you expect your life to be and the way you want it to be. Repeating these statements frequently each day— singing them, saying them silently in your head, feeling the truth of them in your heart, and writing them down over and over—replaces any negative self-talk by re-patterning your brain. You'll begin to feel the potential and possibility of a new reality.

I also have a number of personal affirmations that have become my mantras over the years. I invite you to use these or write yours in your own voice. Just be sure that each statement uses positive wording in the present tense and includes the words "I am." Most importantly, no "buts" allowed!

- ❤ I am following my intuition at all times.
- ❤ I am the source of my own authority.
- ❤ I am approaching life and all that it has to offer with an open heart.
- ❤ I am feeling my way through my decision-making processes.
- ❤ I am open to receiving love, health, happiness, money, and success in everything I do.
- ❤ I am releasing all that no longer serves my highest and best interest, and I am attracting all that does.

## Financial Meditations

Earlier, we learned how to meditate, and I promised we would be coming back to it. Each of the next four PACT chapters concludes with a financial meditation: words that will give you a focus to think and feel into about in quiet observation. I use meditation to focus on all aspects of my life, including financial. I learned Primordial Sound Meditation at The Chopra Center, which taught me to always begin by asking myself these four questions: *Who am I? What do I want? What is my purpose? What am I grateful for?* When filling in the blanks to W*ho am I?*, I respond, "I am the owner of a multi-million-dollar company based on financial wellness that helps people everywhere live the lives they desire."

*What do I want?* I state my desired outcome just like I did with my weight. Today, I run a multi-million-dollar company; however, before I had achieved it, I made it true through my meditation: "I am creating a multi-million-dollar business that brings in more revenue than I can imagine this year and triples the next." I put it out there in my morning and evening meditation, and it became my reality within the next few years and has since multiplied many times over.

You can meditate on your savings goals, debt ceiling, monthly spending, or any aspect of your life you wish to change. Have fun with it. The more you practice, the more you will see how easily it works. Some clients, including Angela, prefer not to include dates or amounts because they do not want to limit their intentions in any way. Angela wants to be expansive and in the moment as much as possible and adjust her life accordingly. Her current intention is, "I choose to increase my cash flow monthly." And she does.

Responding to my meditative questions helps me achieve clarity: *What is my purpose?* To reaffirm my commitment to help people achieve their dreams and live in the present moment as much as possible.

*What am I grateful for?* It is such a privilege and pleasure to respond to this question that my answers are longer every day. These questions align me with a higher energetic vibration, for which I am most appreciative.

When I quietly meditate, I receive more clarity about what my soul desires and what is or is not serving me well at this moment in time. The words might not come in the form of a rational or conscious thought, but as a message and feeling communicated within my brain and body. Carefully observe the emotions that come up for you on this path for your own personal and financial metamorphosis.

## Using Your Intuition

Your natural intuition, your gut feeling, is your very own personal transformation tool. A distant acquaintance insisted that people who operate from intuition and listening to spirit are, in her words, "basically nuts." The truth is, those who do not use every feature that comes with our minds and bodies are missing out. When you buy a new car or computer, you celebrate the gadgets and intriguing extras. Human beings come fully equipped with a goldmine of bonus features and abilities we must tap into to receive the full benefit.

Each and every one of us can access our entire inner landscape of gut feelings. Too many people push aside and ignore odd messages, much to their detriment. Yes, it takes some time and attention to learn to listen to your inner voice and heed your gut reaction, but it could save more than your financial outlook.

One client, Steven, age 47, was scheduled to fly into New York City for business. He'd been having headaches and felt queasy but kept pushing on. As he boarded the plane and took his seat on the flight, his gut told him to turn around and leave. "It was such an intense feeling I had to pay attention." He took a cab to a hospital emergency room—where he was diagnosed with a brain aneurism. Listening to his gut saved his life!

Intuition works best when you find a quiet time in your busy schedule and mentally create a quiet space in your life through meditation, mindfulness, or prayer. One client, Marlene, begins her morning meditations by asking the Universe, "What is it that I need to know today?" Sometimes she hears responses, and other times the answer unfolds during the day. To me, prayer means *talking* to God or the Universe, and meditation is *listening*. Personally, I have created a comfortable, balanced approach using both.

If you find yourself spinning around all the time, unsure of which direction to take, chances are, you're living in Dramaland, talking to too many people to find your conclusions or to justify your position. Recognize when this is the case and instead turn inward to find your answers. You need to trust your gut instincts and know that the real solutions are there. You are *enough.*

Using your intuition fits everyone's budget. It's on call 24 hours a day, fully ready to provide you with the guidance and solace you need. Once you slow down and hear what is in your heart, you might discover your current job is not feeding your soul and it's time to move on. Or you might recognize your current intimate relationship has nothing left to offer you. If this happens, don't panic. Remember, this lifetime is to be enjoyed. It is not a prison sentence. Too many of us stay in jobs that don't energize us or plug along in dysfunctional relationships. These situations drain us of precious inner energy. Tune in to your intuition for some new ideas, and remember, we all have access to infinite possibilities.

## MONEY ENERGIZING TIME:
### Tuning In

**ME TIME**   Clearing your mind gives you time to consider a variety of different ways to tune in to yourself. When we operate only in our heads, we tend to overanalyze things and remain stuck in old, subconscious patterns. When you open the door and begin to trust your intuition, you will receive the answers you seek.

To get started, use whatever technique you like—such as yoga, exercise, nature walks, guided meditation, deep breathing, or mindfulness training—to create a safe space where you can be in your heart instead of your head. Embrace your "aha!" moments as they arise—this is your intuition speaking to you. When you suddenly get an idea, and it feels good and real, make a note of it and commit to taking action. It's likely a solution to the exact problem you've been wrestling with, such as what to do with your job, a worrisome relationship, or even the next steps in your financial future.

Whatever it is that you've been aching to resolve, whether simple or complex, rest assured that the answer is inside you right now—and that it's been there all the time. We all have a natural, intuitive ability with this inner guidance system. Turn to your inner guidance by quietly asking yourself, *What do I want today?* and listen carefully. You can repeat this question as many times as you need to, in order to keep uncovering the answers you seek. Relax, be open to receive, and give thanks for the guidance.

Keep a notebook or paper handy to jot down any ideas you don't want to forget. For me, there's something about taking a pen to paper that solidifies the manifestation. As you discover the best way to calm your mind, body, and soul, your energy can finally flow again. This is where creativity and innovation thrive. New ideas will come to you, and as you take action, create your own new world. Just remember to breathe along the way and enjoy the journey.

## Tapping into Her Own Wisdom

When she was younger, my client Susan, now age 60, had always been told by her father that, since she had married an accountant, she would never have to worry about money or even need to work, that her husband would take care of everything forever. That's not the way things worked out. Approaching retirement, she suddenly found herself facing a marital breakdown.

Years ago, Susan had given up her dreams of a career to raise her three children. She did volunteer work and odd jobs here and there, but nothing that truly fed her soul and spoke to her higher purpose. She thought that one day perhaps she would just help out with her grandkids. Overall, she was a bit complacent in life—until the divorce hit. At that point, she was angry at herself for having listened to her father, rather than honoring her individuality and pursuing her own dreams. She also felt that her husband had let her down. Meanwhile, she was quickly depleting her finances and becoming increasingly frightened about her future.

One day, after we'd been working together for a while, she sat quietly and asked of the Universe, "Now what? What do I need to know? What am I missing?" She reported that she heard this message in her mind: "I am capable of knowing as much about money as men do." Laughing out loud, she wrote this mantra, describing her mission of personal empowerment: "I am regaining my financial personal power. I forgive myself for mistakes I made before becoming empowered and educated. Money is good. I am grateful to have money in excess. I am open to receiving. I give myself permission to love myself enough to allow money to flow into my life, use it wisely, build it, enjoy it, and share it. There truly is plenty to go around."

With this message in her heart and her mind, Susan gained the courage to come to terms with her financial and personal challenges and was able to change her life by changing her mindset and energetic vibration about how life really works. She accepted personal responsibility and also allowed herself to grieve. She knew that if she didn't mourn the loss of her marriage, it would fester inside of her for years to come, and she felt she had wasted enough time not doing what she really wanted to do.

She was ready to claim *Susan* in every way, shape, and form by facing her own dilemmas. The only way she could do that was to first determine what she wanted to create and then take small steps towards that objective each day. Think of a baby who wants to run before he walks. Babies roll over, crawl, pull up on the furniture, and finally scoot along. Susan decided to tackle life without the burden of unacknowledged regrets. She forgave herself for her past, designed her canvas, and began a new life that eventually made her very happy.

Go back to the way in which you use visualization. One of the exercises you can do is to allow yourself to feel what it would be like for everyone in the world to also have the peace and security you do. See people everywhere, healthier and financially stable, having what they need and want, living in peace with their decisions. Truly feel this in your heart and let it fill every cell in your body. Sit with this peaceful feeling until you feel the urge to return to your place in the world.

Now, let's begin your PACT journey.

CHAPTER 4

# P: PICTURING YOURSELF

---

*Engage in life soulfully.*
~PANACHE DESAI

---

The "P" in PACT stands for a crucial first step towards your overall success, yet it involves something you most likely have not done since you were a child: picturing your ideal life. This then is your opportunity to dream outrageous imaginings for you and your loved ones. Do you remember what you wanted to be when you grew up? If you take all the vigor, vitality, and excitement you had in mind for your life at a young age and add to it the benefit of your maturity, experience, education, and ability, what a powerful "you" is set to emerge! Imagine what a relief and pleasure it will be for you, right now, to focus on who you really are at your core and what you really want in your life.

After all, now is the perfect time. Once you work through this first major step of picturing yourself, so many other aspects of your life will begin to fall in place. The challenge is that we've all stopped dreaming. Our lives have become predictably scheduled and monotonous for the sake of efficiency. Now, it's time to get back to some unstructured and spontaneous living.

Picturing and feeling your ideal life starts from the fire in your belly—your strong desire to live with passion and purpose. There are two levels of "picturing." One involves the materialistic things we know we want, such as a comfortable home, vacation, cars, boats, or new clothes. The second level is stored away in your subconscious mind, where you will find your dreams and your soul's purpose— what you've been called to do in this lifetime.

This might be a new concept for you, or you may have had glimpses of this at various times in your life. For example, have you ever been drawn to something and had no idea why? That feeling is your soul directing you, pointing you where you really want to go. The reason we have become so detached from our soul's desires is that we have little unstructured time in our lives. For most of us, our day is preplanned from the minute we wake up until we tuck in for the night, without any free time to dream about our lives.

Between commuting, working, dining, and taking care of the house, our days are jam-packed. Even on weekends, we have so many commitments that it sometimes feels impossible to find personal down time or even quality time with immediate family. Every client tells me he has absolutely no time to listen to his deepest desires. To that I say, "Love yourself enough to make time for you."

When you give yourself time, your heart will remember. Consciously, you may have no clue about your purpose, but on some level, you felt a connection. Perhaps you were drawn to beautiful gardens, certain types of music or dance, accounting, finance, helping children, or coaching. As you read and grow through these pages, consciously pay attention and notice what you are attracted to.

## JULIE'S GEMS:
# Picturing My Life

I learned how to picture my life when I signed up for a four-part program offered by the Women's Business Development Center in Chicago. As a group, we were looking for new ways to brand and present our businesses, integrated with our personalities and personal identities. Everyone enjoyed our instructor, Marypat, so much that at the end of the session, she offered to continue working with five of us once a week—which five of us did for the next two years.

This class is where I learned that most of us try to create our businesses from a competitive standpoint, doing things the so-called "right" way and building on a pre-existing role model. Marypat taught us to stop trying to change ourselves to fill the traditional model taught in business schools. Marypat helped me realize the value of bringing my true self to the table while capitalizing upon both my masculine and feminine qualities. She challenged each of us: "Discover who you are and what you are all about. Let that be who you present to the world, personally and professionally. In essence, simply become your best self."

Step one involved revamping our marketing materials to better define our unique "brand." Being our authentic selves extended to every statement about each of us, including our personal style, accessories, and clothing. She encouraged us to *own* our femininity and stop apologizing for it in business. She showed us that it was important to be well-put-together business owners and allow our inner and outer sexy personalities and confidence to shine through.

That's when I decided to stop wearing a traditional woman's suit to the office. It literally did not suit me, and I hated the look. An image consultant taught me how to buy the right clothes for my body shape. Dressing for success was not a skill I developed growing up as one of 12 children; that's for sure! My goal was to be more accessible and engaging, rather than stuffy. Likewise, I traded in my traditional mahogany desk and stuffy offices for an airy office loft. Before long, I was liberated. The way my office and I look now delivers a very different message from other financial firms.

Once you start the ball rolling, it's magical. I changed my company name and brand from D.C. Financial, Inc., to JMC Wealth Management, Inc. I rewrote and redesigned my marketing materials to include the emotional component of money management—a pretty radical move at the time. I was the only one talking about and promoting emotional and behavioral financial management. I did what I'm asking you to do—to integrate the creative and logical sides of your brain with your heart, adding in the practice of energy-boosting techniques. Your mindset will vibrate to match your new, energetic vibrational level. Don't be surprised if people begin asking you, "What are you doing differently?" Simply smile and let them know you are working on achieving true peace of mind and the highest quality of life. You will feel more alive than ever: lighter, happier, and fully empowered in the present moment.

As I rediscovered my unique identity, I found a link for "business services with a soul." The organization was called Chicago Healers, and Karyn Pettigrew's profile jumped out at me. She is the author of the book, *I Quit!* and owner of the consulting company Beyond Blind

Spots. She became one of the most influential business coaches I have ever been privileged to work with. She had the ability to help me get out of my own way.

I knew I wanted something different, but I couldn't nail down what that was. I had a blind spot. I just knew something had to change. As I worked with Karyn, she took me through exercises that challenged my thought process and forced me to feel my way to the answers by listening for and following my intuition. As they say, when the student is ready, the teacher appears.

## Vision Boarding 2.0, Vision Living

At the time, one of the most helpful things I learned from Karyn was to create a vision board. The challenge came a few years later when I was the vision boarding queen. I had multiple vision boards, and I was monitoring and measuring how I was manifesting things and waiting for those things that hadn't happened yet. I had manifested things like being on Oprah Radio, which, of course, was on one of my first vision boards. This led to doing WGN Radio and many other things. I was hooked.

One day, I met with a mentor of mine, Anne Emerson. She told me, "Julie, I am giving you an assignment that you need to do this week. You need to take every vision board you have ever made, and you have to burn them." Of course, I told her she was nuts, and she just laughed at me, in pure Anne style. I was so confused.

She told me I had become too attached to outcomes and was no longer living in the present moment. I was so driven to accomplish and manifest that I was obsessing, on some level, about my vision boards and whether or not things had become a reality in my life or not. Anne had always steered me in the right direction, but this one I was really questioning. I thought, *Why not? I'll go ahead and burn them, and worst-case scenario, I'll make them again.* What I didn't anticipate was the physiological response I had when I burned them.

That night, I took all my vision boards and went out on my balcony. It was a chilly fall evening, and I had an old flower pot I was going to use as my fire pit. As I started to rip the boards into small pieces and put them into the fire, tears started to fill my eyes. I had no clue what was happening. The more I burned, the more this internal sadness was rising up and coming out.

If you could have seen the look on my family's faces watching me do this! They wanted to help, but I had no clue what was happening to even tell them what was wrong. Anne was right. I felt like I was burning up my dreams, my future, and my reality. I had become hostage to my vision boards. The essence of them trapped me in an illusion that this was living. I was trapped in my own forecasting, hostage to what I was going to manifest by something I decided in the past, not necessarily what I wanted now, in the present moment.

I wasn't creating the space to be fluid and change my mind. It was as if I was in vision board prison and had no clue what was happening to me. I know that many of you out there may have done the same thing, which is not to say vision boarding hasn't served a critical purpose in the past. But what I do now using this tool is to dig down and tune into my heart's desires in the present moment, to things I may not even be conscious of mentally.

Another way to view this is, if you are physically attracted to things or experiences you currently don't have or don't do, it's a sure sign that there is something else you desire. It could be something fancier, such as more lavish vacations, or it could be that you would be more peaceful with a job that doesn't force you to travel so much, or you might love to work from home and take away your commute. The key is to begin to observe what you are drawn to in day-to-day living and look at this vision boarding process as more of a dynamic process of life.

What is important is to watch when you start to edit yourself. If you notice you are drawn to something, just know that you are. Don't judge; don't evaluate why you can or can't have this or do that—just recognize it. Detach from "how" you'll get it. Just start to make a list of those things you are drawn to and begin allowing yourself to experience some of those things, no matter how much out of your comfort level they really are!

I started to notice I would giggle every time I thought of getting a massage, but growing up Irish Catholic, there were lots of judgments around that. Why would you spend your money on something like that? I'd hear people say things like, "Are you comfortable being in a room with someone while you're practically naked?" Whether you are or not, why does it matter, and why would people say these things to me?

Bottom line: it's about what you're drawn to do. You know, it's that feeling you get when you feel excited or when something makes you giggle or puts that little smirk on your face. It could be that you take a vacation you've always wanted, but would have to take a red-eye night flight and have a layover to make the cash flow work. Who cares? As long as you are going to a place you've always wanted to experience, find a way.

One of my dreams was to go to Ireland, where my ancestors are from. I had no idea how that was going to happen. One Sunday I attended mass at Old St. Pat's in downtown Chicago and, on my way out, grabbed a bulletin. During breakfast, I started to read the bulletin. In the ad section, there was my opportunity to go abroad. It stated, "Raise $2,500 for The Arthritis Foundation, and you get free air fare and hotel to Ireland and entry into the Dublin Marathon."

First and foremost, I had never run a marathon before. Second, I was really good at raising money. So away I went. I started to train and raised the money. I also agreed to raise $1,000 in addition so I could bring my mom along as well. It was 1998, my dream was coming true, and I was headed to the Emerald Isle at no financial cost to myself or to my mom. There is always a way to put yourself where you desire to be. You just have to be willing to think it's a possibility and have the courage to do something about it in the present moment.

Keep in mind that it may feel odd; you may feel out of place when you go do the things you don't normally do, such as get a massage, hang out at a place you've dreamed of spending time in, surround yourself with people who have accomplished things you want to accomplish, or vacation to a foreign country. It's about just doing it. The more you do, the more you begin to feel like you've been doing it for a lifetime. You need to just get over the initial jitters. You can live a dynamic life with constant "vision living" by continuously expanding your frequency through going out of your comfort level regularly and consistently.

## Integrating the Power of Your Brain

Now that you've had some fun with the vision living exercise, let's look at why this works. We have two sides to our brains for a reason. They complement each other, and we need to use them both. (See figure 3.)

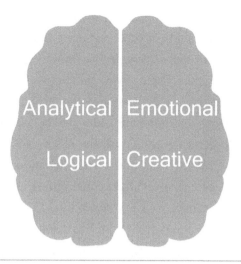

Decision Making Order

1st Emotional

2nd Analytical

Figure 3: Left Brain vs. Right Brain

Vision living integrates both sides of yourself. Through living this way, I have tapped into my heart and subconscious mind on the all-important right side of my brain, where creativity resides. I became more balanced, and my *own* creativity extended into other areas of my life. For example, I found myself being more innovative than ever while working with clients to find viable solutions to some very difficult situations. I was constantly being challenged with increasingly difficult scenarios, testing my belief that the PACT system could help anyone get from where they were to where they wanted to be.

My right brain, in conjunction with my heart space, combined with my logical, analytical left brain, to find the answers. What a team!

You can do this too by digging deep into your subconscious mind, integrating your heart and your head, and bringing your soul's desires, your authentic self, to the surface. In the same way that I needed to exercise my creative brain, those of you right brainers who hate dealing with finances and money need to exercise your analytical side.

But using your non-dominant side can be challenging. It is important to stop carrying around all the shame and guilt that you don't "understand money" and allow your money understanding to grow. As both sides of your mind get equal billing and become fully integrated, you'll discover your full capabilities. Vision living works so well because the feelings from your heart and the images in your subconscious mind rise to the surface. Your reasoning skills are not involved.

Usually when we consider doing something, we try to reason out why it works or doesn't work. With vision living, all you do is capture what you are drawn to. The process of vision living takes out the "why" and "what" and "how" factors. At this point in the process, there's no need to know why or how; all you need is the attraction. It's as if you've circumvented your left brain completely. The theory behind vision living is integration, leading with your heart and integrating with your mind. The very inspirational Gregg Braden and the Heart Math Institute discipline have been two of my greatest teachers in this area.

As you follow the PACT steps, you will see glimpses into the future you've dreamed of and pictured, but were unable to achieve previously. Don't be surprised if, along the way, you begin to release sorrow for mistakes in the past. Focus on achieving your goals, coming out of your cocoon, and unloading old emotions, things, and people in your life that are weighing you down. You'll transition to the career path and lifestyle that really feed your soul.

## Tapping into Brain Waves

Once you visualize what you want, tapping into your brain waves can be a powerful tool to reinforce what you have visualized. None of us want to suffer or make things harder on ourselves; it's the subconscious mind that plays havoc with our lives. Our subconscious mind is where our beliefs are stored. Our core beliefs include love, self-worth, wholeness, and safety. How we respond to the world around us comes from what we hold on to within the subconscious mind.

To help people reach deeper inside themselves, I refer my clients to websites where they can listen to and download very specific meditative music that positively impacts brain wave patterns; it elevates their energetic vibration. In so doing, they are able to create mental space that allows the *new* in their lives to formulate and take root. This works so well because, according to scientists and neurologists, everyone has five brain waves: Beta, Alpha, Theta, Delta, and Gamma.

The first four are well-known, but Gamma is less well understood. Each has its own frequency, measured in cycles per second (Hz). Beta waves are associated with being awake; they help you function. Alpha is the relaxation wave to ride while dreaming, relaxing, or meditating. Theta waves appear during deep meditation and REM dreaming. The products I recommend are programmed to the Theta brain wave pattern to reach the subconscious and re-pattern it. Think of it as reframing the words you use. Instead of using the word *hope*, you *trust*. It reframes what your desired outcome is. These brain wave meditations do the same thing. As opposed to reframing, they *re-pattern* your belief system. Being "in Theta" means achieving a spiritual connection with the Universe. Beyond that, your Delta brain wave frequency is achieved when you enter deep sleep or transcendental meditation.

Researchers report that there is a sweet spot on the Alpha-Theta wavelength border where visualization, creativity, and mind programming take place, creating your waking reality. If you wish to try this technique, I suggest you find a store online, such as Brain Sync® (www.brainsync.com). Scroll down the shopping list of MP3s and CDs offered. Focus on the album covers that jump off the screen at you. Typically, I find that clients will come up with about four to six titles that really stand out. I ask them to select the most prominent one that speaks to them, because that is the one their soul wants to work on, first and foremost.

These titles are inexpensive to purchase online and are available for immediate download or on CD. All you need do is put on your headphones as you are going to sleep and allow the tones, sounds, and words to do their work. I don't know anyone who actually stays awake for the duration. No worries, though—the work is completed while you are sleeping in the Theta brain wave. What great time management!

## JULIE'S GEMS:
## Shifting from the Inside Out

Never underestimate the power you have to control your destiny. When we picture something we passionately desire and focus all our energy and intention on it and express gratitude that it has already happened, we can manifest anything we choose, in all aspects of our lives. Once I saw the intense power of shifting my own energy, I realized this could be applied to every aspect of my life.

Eight years ago, I wanted more than anything to have my second child, Bridget, using natural childbirth, not another C-section, which is what I had to have with my first child. Timmy's delivery by C-section was not a good experience for me, to say the least. When I got pregnant the second time, I was terrified that this would happen again. I had been successful in many other areas in my life, but failed at natural childbirth. This second time, I was incredibly motivated to have a natural birth experience. The cards were stacked against me because most medical professionals have a protocol that after a C-section, this shouldn't be attempted. However, I felt pretty confident that the energetic and universal principles I used in business and in life could help me to achieve this goal.

That's not to say it was easy. One of my biggest challenges was figuring out how to overcome my usual left brain logic and follow my heart's desire—the one I pictured for myself and this little miracle soon to be born. Logic told me the medical people were against me trying it, so I set out to find allies who could help me manifest natural birth this time around. I was very fortunate to get excellent advice from my OB's nurse, Lisa Phillips. When I was pregnant with Bridget, she knew what I was dreaming of and said to me, "Julie, if you want to succeed at this, you have to throw away that birth plan in your purse—the one I know is in there. Just get out of your head and get into your body. Let your body do what it knows how to do, and stop trying to control it all."

Another example of body intelligence I mentioned earlier is that our bodies are smarter than our minds; we just need to listen. Lisa's sage advice pushed me to try something I had never tried before. I was very interested in tapping into my own brain waves and had actually purchased a set of CDs from Kelly Howell at Brain Sync® years ago, but never listened to them. The Howell track that captured my attention was "Desire," so every night during my pregnancy, I listened to the "Desire" MP3 download until I fell asleep. I believe this technique taught me how to hold on strongly to my own desires and boundaries and overcome my logical, analytical side, which had the potential to sabotage my efforts.

It worked! I had a successful natural delivery with Bridget. I had faced and overcome all my fears through visualizing and felt the way I expected to feel after having a successful outcome. While listening to the CD, I saw this healthy baby, Bridget Marie, as she came into the world. I felt the joy of her arriving without surgery, and I gave thanks for her natural birth to Dr. Brian Foley and his team, my doulas Barb and Jacque, and everyone else who supported me—even before I knew for sure it would come to pass.

Moving back to PACT, what do all these warm and fuzzy moments have to do with financials? I wanted to illustrate to you how you can overcome the deepest fears, personal blocks, and even widely held scientific beliefs by using the power of your intention and your desire. It helps when you can override your logical mind, which is busy telling you such a belief is ridiculous. This system works because once you can picture something with complete clarity, you begin to feel something happening in every cell of your body.

If you are completely grateful for it, your mind can absolutely overcome matter. I am living proof. This is why I say you can never dream too big. The other reason that worked in my favor was I didn't allow myself to buy in to all the unreasonable fears in my head and in those around me about it *not* being possible. Instead, I faced my fears and sought out the kinds of techniques that would quiet my noisy subconscious mind.

## Face the Music to Change the Future

As insights and new directions come into your conscious mind, bravely face any fears you have about change. It's really hard to look at, let alone admit, that something you've done, created, or said in your life has not served you well. For example, for years I used money as a tool to buy love, through taking friends and family to dinner, buying them presents, and even bailing them out of financial chaos. Once I exchanged money or gifts with the other person, I set expectations as to how I expected her to show up for me in my life. Time and time again, I was disappointed. My expectations were never met. When I became conscious that this had nothing to do with the individuals and in actuality only had to do with me, I was really sad.

At that point I had a choice. I could continue trying to buy love, or I could use my newly found knowledge to create healthier relationships. Think of it this way: We've all heard stories of a person who has faced a personal crisis or near death experience and emerged with a new determination to make his remaining life span more meaningful and enjoyable. Through meditation, visualization, or using brain-wave music therapy, you have that same kind of objective opportunity to observe and discover your magnificent self. It's time to look in the mirror and say, "I'm ready to see what I've been hiding from."

We are all sending intentions out into the world. But when we do, what is it we are attracting? Remember the push and pull? One way to view this is that whenever you stop pushing your opinions on others, the real healing begins. When you stop the push, the next step is to quiet your mind so your ego doesn't dominate your existence. Then you can allow your heart to rise to the occasion.

Our hearts don't lie, nor do our bodies. Our own body intelligence sends us messages all the time. You can recognize these messages by feeling physical pain or emotional turmoil throughout your system. Once you learn to recognize and trust your gut instinct, you'll realize it doesn't matter what anyone else says. It's okay to be where you are, regardless of what others think. Perhaps they are the ones who are unconscious, not you.

Taking time for introspection and self-care allows you to remain aware that your net worth is a reflection of your self-worth. We are all deserving. The net worth you create is a manifestation of how much you love yourself and of your desire to live a life of Abundance. Net worth can be measured in dollars or cash flow, but also in an Abundance of time and freedom in your life. It's what you define net worth to be, not only the actual monetary resources.

## MONEY ENERGIZING TIME:
## Brainstorming Your Future

**ME TIME**   This exercise is best done if you approach the questions with an open mind and loving heart. Shut down any blame, shame, guilt, and judgments, and allow yourself to fill in the particulars of your ideal life. This exercise will help you change your response system and enable you to say, "Yes, that has been my pattern, but it's behind me now." It's OK to acknowledge where you've been, while refusing to slide backwards ever again.

Become a dream maker. First and foremost, allow your dreams to rise to the surface, where they can serve as your impetus for change. Continue brainstorming through each of the following questions, expanding your answers as you go. Be as specific in your responses as you possibly can because it's best to avoid generalities. If answers are not coming, take a deep breath and repeat the question. Soon a space will open in your mind to hear the answer. There's no right or wrong way here. Just stick with it, stay focused, and keep breathing.

BRAINSTORMING YOUR FUTURE:
## Questions to Consider:

- Where would you like to see yourself in three to five years? Include any elements that come to mind about life, including work, family, financial, or personal life.
- What are your coworkers like? What is your boss like? If you are self-employed, what is your workday like?
- At your job, what would you love to do daily? Is that what you did today at work?
- Why did you choose your current career path? Does it excite you today?
- When you were a child, what were your dreams? What makes you joyful today?
- What have you always wanted to do? Do you have any regrets?
- What desires have you been negotiating away due to "life circumstances"?
- From a family life perspective, what have you always been drawn to?
- What is on your back-burner? What keeps you from doing it?
- Do people tell you that you are crazy for thinking the way you do? Great! That means you're really close to having it all.
- What physical ailments or mental blocks concern you?

These ailments are excellent signs of what needs to be addressed first. Think of ways you can visualize your life without any blocks or health concerns. They will usually start to melt away anyway once you step into your true purpose.

As you record these answers and think about what you'd really like to do, notice your physical responses. Do you feel nervous? Are you biting your nails? This may indicate you're afraid to move forward. During your childhood or early adult years, did someone you love and respect tell you not to bother even thinking about your dream job? Were you told your dream job was fiscally irresponsible? Are you crossing your arms now to protect your heart space?

As you begin to become more aware of the reactions in your body, mind, and spirit, you will see these are signs you are getting ready to make changes that can transform your life. You are closer than ever to finding the solutions to move forward. Keep the brainstorming processes going. It's quite possible that the "old story" you used to tell yourself will creep up on occasion, wreaking havoc on your new path. Notice it, then move away from what has been holding you back for so long.

To continue brainstorming, continually ask yourself, *What more can I add about what I love? What else do I need to know? What else do I desire at this moment in time?* Close your eyes, take a deep breath in, let it out, and continue asking, *What else?* Typically, answers will pop right into your head. If your response takes more than 30 seconds to process, then you are still operating from your logical, left-brain side. Don't edit yourself.

These exercises are all about fully expressing your needs. Keep going and eventually your left-brain, logical side will be sidelined and quieted. It doesn't matter how crazy or unobtainable it may seem, just let your heart do the talking and let your old life stories do the walking—right out of your life.

Have faith and trust that whatever you write down is completely possible. Understand that your left brain can be a tough cookie to quiet down. Be patient. It will come. Just keep trying and creating the space for your deepest desires to come to the surface. One of my personal coaches, Dierdre Morgan, says, "Think with an expanded mind and an expressive heart. Start with your heart, then add your smarts."

## A Must-Have Conversation

The first question I ask all of my clients is what I just asked you: "Where would you like to see yourself in three to five years?" Clients respond, "You mean financially?" I say, "It doesn't matter; wherever you would like to start is fine." Clients never start the discussion about money. It's always what they want personally, professionally, or in their family life.

Ultimately, the process I walk them through is about living fully. Sometimes clients want to talk about travel or perhaps focus more on their health. The conversation hardly ever includes money because we don't put it in the same category as home, health, and well-being, yet these are all dependent upon currency. Unfortunately, we do not regard money—as we should—as a tangible, relatable force in our life, one that we have the power to control.

Next, I always ask the following questions:

- ♥ Why do you want these things or experiences?
- ♥ What's your driver?
- ♥ What do you love?
- ♥ What would make you happy?
- ♥ What makes you smile?
- ♥ What feels life-supporting?
- ♥ What makes you feel alive and energized?"

The answers to these questions all reside in your heart space. That's where the golden answers wait for your discovery.

## Just Like Oprah

An excited client called as he walked out of *Oprah Live!* "Oprah gives the same advice that you do, to live a heart-centered life." He was so enthusiastic. "She said to go back to your oldest memory of when you were a child, of what you were really passionate about.

What was that? Now let's start living from this passionate, heart-centered place."

Sometimes something really hits us hard when we hear it from someone else. I, too, challenge you to picture yourself in your own passionate place, doing and living what you totally love.

## MONEY ENERGIZING TIME:
## Exploring Your Future from All Angles

**ME TIME** We can plan ahead for our future in the same way as we can break our finances down into small, manageable pieces. Working with clients, I help divide their future by identifying four areas:

1. Financial Life
2. Work Life
3. Personal Life
4. Family Life

Let's use the techniques we learned earlier in our financial questionnaire. Keep the responses for each area of your life on separate sheets of paper. Ask yourself each question three times, regarding your work, personal life, family life, and financial life:

- ♥ When thinking about (work, personal, financial, and family), what are your most immediate thoughts?
- ♥ How do you feel?
- ♥ Do certain words or responsibilities make you uncomfortable?
- ♥ Do you get excited or energized by where you are now?

- Is there something missing in your work, personal, financial, or family life?
- Do you long for or seek something else?
- Can you describe what you are looking for?
- What would you most love to change about your job, personal, financial, or family life?
- What else?

Remember, these are not yes or no, good or bad. They simply are. They are you. Be honest and keep drilling down to provide more details wherever you can. Search your heart and soul for what aspects of your life suit you now. Once your lists are complete, be sure to add timeframes to each entry. Your answers will help you move through the PACT process.

## MONEY ENERGIZING TIME:
## Choosing Your Career Path

**ME TIME**   We spend so many hours working that we really need to be intentional with what we want in that arena. Brainstorming your desired professional life will help you attract the following:

1. people who energize and appreciate you
2. the ideal salary you deserve
3. the quality of life you seek

Articulate all the details you can on how your calling makes you feel, day in and day out. Stay out of your head and follow your heart.

## Work Life Brainstorming Questions:

- Is your current role in your company feeding your soul?
- If money did not matter, what would you be doing instead?
- What total income do you want to make in your new position?
- What kind of person will your new boss be?
- What values does your new employer possess?
- What is the culture of the company?
- How many hours per week do you want to work?
- How many vacation days per year do you want?
- What types of bonuses do you seek?
- Do you want a company stock option as part of your compensation package? Explain why or why not.
- What type of physical atmosphere do you want?
- Do you want the flexibility to work from home or other locations?
- Do you want to travel with your job? If so, how much?
- What type of people do you want to serve with the work you do?
- Do you prefer to not interact with clients?
- Do you want to work in an office, with your hands, out in the field, with the end customer, or on the design side?
- What career path opportunities are you looking for?
- What quality of life characteristics are important to you in your job? How would they show up for you?
- Do you work better alone or in a collaborative setting?
- What qualities do you seek in your team members?
- Do you want to build your own dream, or are you great at supporting others to achieve theirs?
- Do you have the entrepreneurial itch?
- What business opportunities are you attracted to?

**ME TIME**

MONEY ENERGIZING TIME:
## Enjoying Life to the Fullest

## Personal Life Brainstorming Questions:

- ♥ Do you want to travel? Where would you like to go?
- ♥ Are you at your ideal weight?
- ♥ Would you like to improve your overall health and well-being? What do you need to do to achieve this?
- ♥ What makes you feel alive?
- ♥ What foods and exercise best feed your physical body?
- ♥ Is your current diet plan feeding your well-being?
- ♥ Are you in tune with your body's intelligence? If yes, what do you hear it telling you?
- ♥ Do you listen to and learn from your body?
- ♥ Sometimes it's best to let your hairdresser cut your hair without having a game plan. Be open to possibilities. Can you let go of control long enough to let her?
- ♥ What makes you feel fresh, new, more alive, and vibrant?
- ♥ When was the last time you bought yourself clothes that made you feel fabulous?
- ♥ When was the last time you went dancing?
- ♥ Would you like to go dancing?
- ♥ What do you do for fun?
- ♥ What would you *like* to do to have more fun?
- ♥ Do you plan for leisure or unstructured time? Do you want to?
- ♥ What would your calendar look like if you had more downtime?
- ♥ Do you desire more alone time?
- ♥ Would you like to have more social time?
- ♥ What do you need to change to rebalance your life?

- Do you need time to recharge your batteries? If so, when is the most ideal time to do so?
- Do you retain friendships that no longer work for you?
- Do you want to move from negative relationships to more supportive ones?
- Are there people in your life who drive you crazy? Does that work for you?
- Are you looking for companionship? If yes, describe that person, all aspects.
- Are your friendships mutually beneficial?
- Do you have supportive people in your life? If yes, do you feel you get the support you need, or are you seeking a new personal board of directors?
- Are there any hobbies you've wanted to explore?
- Are there any classes you want to take?
- When was the last time you took an adventure?
- If you've had an adventure recently, what is your next great adventure?

## MONEY ENERGIZING TIME:
## Your Ideal Family Life Situation

ME TIME

## Family Life Brainstorming Questions

- Would you like to get married?
- Are you doing the things that will position yourself to be "lucky" to meet that special someone?
- Do you want to get divorced?
- Are you considering a divorce and need to spend time alone to gain some clarity?
- Do you want children?
- What does your family life look like in your ideal world?

- ♥ Would you consider adopting or other family-building options?
- ♥ Would you consider being a single parent, or will you parent only with a partner?
- ♥ Do you want to spend more time with your children or grandchildren?
- ♥ Do you plan activities that are mutually enjoyable for all of you?
- ♥ Does your significant other want the same things you do?
- ♥ Do you live your life to the fullest? If not, why?
- ♥ Despite the number of years you've spent with your partner, do you still want the same things in your life, moving forward?
- ♥ Are you questioning your sexual orientation or identity?
- ♥ Do you need to distance yourself from your parents or siblings?
- ♥ Do you want to have a closer relationship with your immediate family?
- ♥ If you do or don't have a relationship with your siblings or their spouses, do you or do you not want to find ways to connect with your nieces and nephews?
- ♥ How do you define family?
- ♥ Does your family include blood relatives only or close friendships too?
- ♥ Do you spend holidays with family members who stress you out?
- ♥ How would you spend your time for an ideal holiday?
- ♥ Would you consider planning out your holidays your way, no ifs, ands, or buts?
- ♥ Do you feel fiscally responsible for family members?
- ♥ Is it your pleasure, or a source of resentment, handing money out to others?
- ♥ Are you dependent upon family money or inheritance?

- ♥ What goals do you have to secure a career that will fully support you?
- ♥ Do you want to move physically farther away from family to create space?
- ♥ Do you interact with your family as you think you "should" or on your own terms?
- ♥ Do you know how to create healthy boundaries?
- ♥ Would you welcome more interaction with your family?
- ♥ Can you set up dates and activities that work best for you and your family to get together?

## Processing Your Answers and Moving Forward

Once you answer these questions honestly, allow yourself to review and reflect on your responses, highlighting the main themes. Put a star beside the points that surprise and please you. See how themes overlap from the different lists, indicating a possible alignment. For questions that seem to only call for a yes or no, add "then what," and think about what changes you might need to make in that arena.

If you haven't done so, add timelines to the important objectives you really want to accomplish, in order to prioritize them. Then create a plan of action, one step at a time, to work toward what you want and intend to manifest. Be ambitious and, once again, don't worry about *how* you will get there. The Universe will help you.

Here is what you do want to do: for each of the important questions above, where you want more or better results, begin to actively use the techniques we have been discussing in this chapter. Begin to identify and dispel limiting beliefs by taking action steps towards replacing each one with your newly chosen reality. Using energy shifting techniques, regularly and consistently, is the most powerful way to effect changes in your life.

Consider which techniques you feel will be most effective for you: affirmations, vision living, guided visualizations, meditation, or putting personal action plans into place. Whichever resonates with you (some or all) is what you should do, on a consistent basis. Only visualizing or meditating once a month doesn't do it. Life is dynamic in nature, so you need to keep the reinforcements going. The techniques you use regularly serve to reinforce what is in your heart space and inform the Universe of your intentions.

We will be discussing additional energy modalities. I encourage you to be relentless in claiming and then living by your new intentions. The clearer your objectives, the more likely you are to receive back. If at this time you're not very clear, fine! Continue refining and clarifying your intention. It's all good. I constantly remind myself, "Julie, it will happen in divine time, not Julie time."

Let's close out this chapter by using your visualization skills. To acquire abundant reality, you must see it, experience it, feel it deeply as if it is already yours, and express gratitude for it. Becoming abundant begins with wanting or doing something different, something other than what you already have or experienced. This is your compelling reason to change. The responses you have to these exercises lead you into your future. Mentally and energetically, you can resonate with Abundance rather than be stuck again in the Hybrid. Choose Abundance with all of your focused intention and energy. The personal rewards and satisfaction are endless.

## MONEY ENERGIZING TIME:
### Tips to Move Yourself Forward

ME TIME  Remember, when you speak of or picture your ideal life, you are, in essence, designing a life in perfect alignment with your soul. This is a process, and our personalities—our egos—constantly try to get in the way.

To prevent this from occurring, let's review the important action steps you need to take in order to significantly boost your ability to picture your ideal life:

- Use your right brain to visualize and feel into what is your ideal life. If limiting beliefs and fears begin to overwhelm you, recognize the left brain is creating interference that you can and must ignore.
- Focus on the life-enhancing elements in your life, which are supported by your choices.
- Be a seeker as you research various resources and techniques to help you clear away your limiting beliefs and address unwanted subconscious patterns.
- Replace the thought, *I am not worthy of a life of financial Abundance*, with the verbal declaration, "I am worthy and living a life of financial Abundance."
- Participate in events that enable you to learn more about those things that make you excited about life.
- Identify people who live abundantly and excel at cash flow management. Emulate the traits you admire in them.
- Surround yourself with people who support what you want to create in your life now, based on your new story.
- Listen to music, read books, and watch television programs and films that reflect the new pathways in your brain.

## Acting Out Two Different Scripts

Within a marriage or partnership, remaining balanced as a couple can be challenging. Kristine consulted with me because of her awareness that she had an Abundance mentality and her husband Karl did not. She wanted to explore the possibility of shifting his thinking toward an Abundance framework.

In our first session, Karl was skeptical about our being able to accomplish this. He had a very masculine, logical, and analytical approach to everything. In contrast, Kristine was heart-centered and thoughtful, applying her internal feminine energy to her finances and her life. They both firmly believed they were right in their approach. Fortunately, I was able to help them reach a workable compromise.

In our first meeting, I was very surprised when Kristine came clean. Although it initially appeared that she lived by her own financial truth, she was not living authentically. She had accumulated $40,000 in credit card debt that her husband did not know about. Since we were not yet meeting with her husband, Kristine frantically begged me to help her to somehow expand the household budget so she could pay down the debt without his finding out.

At our next meeting, it became clear that neither spouse resonated with an Abundance mentality. They were caught trying to control each other—using cash flow as a power play. Karl wanted the power and control and thought he had won through trying to convince her to see things his way. Instead, his strategy had backfired, and he was ultimately disempowered by his wife's $40,000 debt.

The better solution, right from the start, would have been to honestly admit they had no intention of meeting halfway. Instead, they tried tricking each other into believing they were cooperating—while continuing their own controlling games. This relates to our next chapter, "Awakening Your Authenticity," and to the need for living within the truth of authenticity every day in every way. Kristine never intended to follow Karl's plan, while he believed she was following him. They clearly needed to collaborate on the ideal life they each wanted to live and blend their two worlds.

We worked well together for the next few years. With Karl, we stuck to the numbers, while Kristine was more interested in strategizing and improving her Abundance mentality. They both did their homework. We aligned their finances to support their desired life, and they reported doing well together. They were able to work through many of their problems, validating their different points of view.

## Accepting Your Reality

You are the only person who can design and lead your life. At times, it may feel like you are reacting more than deciding. However, every decision you make changes how you live. To be the head designer of your own life, it's critical you quiet the left or linear brain, because that's the bossy side, commandeering your thoughts with weighty evaluations. By making yourself your priority, you tap into your creative right brain, feeling what's true for you and living from your heart-based core.

Your left brain thinking may try to judge and over-evaluate every step you take, but just acknowledge those warnings without giving them energy and keep dreaming and brainstorming. Try your best to remain calm, centered, excited, relieved, and happy, completely grounded in the present moment, where the most effective brainstorming will occur.

Don't be surprised if your left brain continues interrupting with all of the reasons why you can't have what you want. Have faith that your roadmap will appear to show you how to proceed through the PACT process to the end of your personal rainbow and the real wealth that awaits. In the final stage of PACT, you will learn how to prioritize your actions. For now, the next step is "Accepting Your Reality and Awakening Your Authenticity." Let's continue together on our path!

 ## Financial Meditation

*I am living a life of financial abundance and inner peace. It fits. It feels good. I release and let go of any discomfort. My purpose defines my beliefs, and my beliefs*

*lead to my actions. I picture my ideal life clearly and send out supportive intentions. I am in the flow, giving and receiving, in the fullness of life. I am comfortable making decisions and actions to achieve my dreams and goals for the future.*

Addendum for couples: *I am collaborating openly with my spouse or partner. Both of us are fully open to achieving the dreams and goals we identified for our future together.*

**CHAPTER 5**

# A: ACCEPTING YOUR REALITY AND AWAKENING YOUR AUTHENTICITY

*Authenticity is a collection of choices that we have to make every day. It's about the choice to show up and be real. The choice to be honest. The choice to let our true selves be seen.*

~ BRENÉ BROWN

You have pictured yourself where you want to be in life. Now it's time to learn how to accept your reality and awaken your authenticity. Self-acceptance is about acknowledging exactly who you are and where you are right now. Authenticity comes with knowing who you are and what you want in your own life. Living as your authentic self will fuel your success.

In this chapter, you will determine your operational financial foundation and identify the patterns in your life that have brought

**103**

you there. Some common repetitions include not wanting to open financial statements, having credit or debit card dependency, or feeling an aversion to using cash. Being a workaholic can also work against you. It's a common, socially acceptable way to distract ourselves from problems we don't want to confront.

You might initially feel insecure and doubt yourself because you have not been functioning as "your true you" for a long time. Throughout your lifetime, being attuned to yourself can come and go like the ocean's tides. Simply becoming aware of these small chinks in your new armor will help you remain on your PACT path. You have within you all you need to weather any ups and downs and become your own personal hero on this journey.

As we continue working through the PACT process, many emotions will rise to the surface. Let's begin by meeting Victoria, a woman who struggled to accept her reality and awaken her authenticity.

## Hold on to Your Personal Power

Victoria, age 40, decided she'd had enough of her miserable marriage. When we met, she was newly separated and battling to put money into her name. She experienced great sadness when one child opted to stay with the father, but otherwise things were coming together.

She was well-educated with a six-figure income and could support the lifestyle she chose. She built her financial plan, purchased a condominium, went on vacations, remodeled her home, and saved for her children's college, all the while solidifying her own retirement savings.

As Victoria created space in her life for peace and happiness, she was open to a new relationship. The man she met seemed perfect and everything was going very well. They traveled the world and loved their time together. Her children and his from a previous marriage were all young adults.

Victoria said she wanted me to meet him to help them start building a life together. In reality, she wanted me to convince him they should both sell their homes to buy a new place. This is where her plans began to unravel.

We ran the numbers for their lifestyle and retirement goals. While the new plans looked good on paper, he remained unwilling to sell the home where he and his ex-wife had lived. He had all kinds of excuses, which showed he was not as committed to their new life as she was. When I pointed this out, she refused to accept my observations.

Over the next few years, I watched as she gave up parts of herself, piece by piece, to be in the relationship. He was adept at holding his own personal boundaries, and she continued folding. They went on the trips he wanted, and she sold her condo to move in with him. They fought over how to remodel the home to make it their own. He was completely shut off from the emotional side of what she was trying to create. His refusal to change in any way sabotaged their new life. She continued seeing me, but he stopped.

At our last appointment, she was wearing new glasses because she was going legally blind. I asked her, "What is it in your life that you do not want to see?" I could see it clear as day. She was creating the same life with this second man that she had with her first husband, giving away too much of herself for the sake of the relationship. Her actions were based on a deep-seated fear of being alone.

I was disappointed but not surprised when she told me she wasn't going to work with me anymore because they were getting married and he wanted to manage all of their money. I worried for her, but it was her choice to give in to fear instead of awakening her authentic self.

Her story should be a wake-up call for everyone. I see this scenario unfold far too often. We give up our power because we think the other person knows what's best. My advice to any woman or man caught up in giving away too much of your personal power is to stop immediately.

If you only take one message away from this book, it should be this: hold on to your own power and do not allow fear to undermine who you truly are. When you do your work and address your fears and limiting beliefs head-on, you will reap huge rewards. While Victoria had to spend the last half of her life figuring out her money and personal issues, some people change much more quickly.

## Reality Check

Josie, age 37, understood PACT immediately and decided to change her life, practically overnight. She arrived in my office about one year after losing her office job, which entailed leading a sales management team. There had been plenty of warning signals that she needed to find a new job, but she waited too long to take action. She was laid off before properly preparing for a transition and processed the stress of losing her job by overspending and living on her savings and retirement money.

When jobs in your established career are not coming to you easily, it can be a message to shift gears. Josie was forced to look more broadly, felt a calling to seek a very different career direction, and jumped into a new adventure in real estate.

As the synchronicities of life occur, a realtor in her office was a client of mine. Josie walked into my office open to change—something I rarely ever see in a first visit. It was refreshing because my words and advice resonated with her, especially when we discussed how to use her money to fund the life she wanted.

Since she was already off and running in her new career, the income side was solving itself, but we needed to uncover the "whys" behind her overspending. She rented a home shared with roommates, but home ownership was one of the compelling incentives for her to take charge of her finances. Together, we mapped out her debt and monthly cash flow, and we set up goals for intentional spending on a desired vacation and on owning her own home.

We also shaped a creative retirement plan with income generated through rental real estate. Her goal was to acquire five properties to provide the bulk of her retirement income and then the balance was to be built upon other pre-existing assets. Josie took every recommendation to heart and jumped in with both feet, surrendering to PACT. We also explored her personal dreams, career goals, and family relationships.

Josie was mindful not to engage with old patterns of spending or debt. She accepted the life she lived before, and without guilt weighing her down, she went on to make conscious and deliberate changes. She could have been highly self-critical because she was still single, had meager savings, and felt too old to still be renting an apartment. Working with the PACT process got her past that.

Despite ups and downs, in less than a year she manifested the income from house sales and bought a condominium with space to attract the man she wanted in her life. This was by far the fastest manifestation I have ever seen. She released her past and trusted she would receive 100 percent of what she desired—and she did!

## MONEY ENERGIZING TIME:
### It's Your Turn

**ME TIME**    Let's clarify your financial picture:

- ♥ Gather all of your statements and financial information in one place.
- ♥ Record debt, money coming in, money going out, and assets.
- ♥ Add up each column with totals along the bottom. (See figure 4.)

| Past | Present | Future |
| --- | --- | --- |
| Debt | Cash Flow | Assets |

Figure 4: Financial Timeline

Start a fresh page in your notebook to track the following:

- Daily expenses
- Weekly expenses
- Bills paid monthly
- Annual bills: don't forget to include these as they really can throw cash flow for a loop when they are due. (See figure 5.)

| Daily Expenses | Weekly Expenses | Annual Bills |
|---|---|---|
|  |  |  |
|  |  |  |
|  |  |  |
|  |  |  |
|  |  |  |

### Bills Paid Monthly

| Housing |  |
|---|---|
| Mortgage / Rental | $ |
| HOA & Maintenance | $ |
| Utilities | $ |
| Property Taxes | $ |
| Housing Total | $ |

| Transportation |  |
|---|---|
| Loan / Lease | $ |
| Fuel | $ |
| Service | $ |
| Insurance | $ |
| Transportation Total | $ |

| Medical Expenses |  |
|---|---|
| Medical | $ |
| Dental | $ |
| Medications | $ |
| Medical Total | $ |

| Totals | $ |
|---|---|

Figure 5: Your Cash flow

Regardless of income, it's the expense side that will create problems. Learning to consistently say no to things that are not in alignment with healthy financial living is the key. Keep a small notebook in your pocket to record all of the money you spend, from a subway MetroCard to the daily newspaper, coffee, muffin, or lunch. The process of writing down your cash expenses will help you internalize the action of your cash flow as it comes in and goes out. Be sure to also add any personal debt payments to the equation.

That's not an easy accomplishment. However, it's a necessary step toward financial security. I can't tell you how many people walk into my office with unopened banking and investment statements out of fear of what might be inside. Avoidance does not make anything disappear—it simply delays the inevitable. Monetary realities are just like our emotions: we have to identify and process through them. Once you have everything in one place, summarized, and added up, take a deep breath and review the numbers. Accept the truth without judgment or scorn. It is what it is. Be proud of yourself for your own personal reconciliation. In chapter 6, we will evaluate a variety of financial patterns and will refer back to your daily spending records. Keep tracking your cash flow, growth, and daily improvements.

One of my clients, Carol, a certified public accountant working in property appraisal, has a great system. She does all of her banking online but keeps an old fashioned checkbook register in her pocketbook, with her current bank balance up-to-date. Every time she uses cash or a credit or debit card, she writes the entry in and deducts it from her balance. It keeps her bottom line in check.

## Your Economic Choice Point

Our goal is to determine how you approach money and spending. The responsibility belongs to each of us to understand and accept Your Economic Choice Point©. The good news is that if you don't like your current set point, you can consciously alter and reinforce it with your daily behaviors. The PACT process replaces old patterns that no longer work for you with new financial models that will. Let's look at the Economic Choice Point (figure 6) chart.

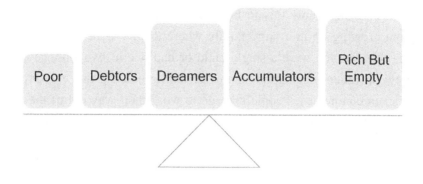

Figure 6: Economic Choice Point

To figure out where you stand, read through the descriptions. Look at the choice points for both you and your spouse or partner. As you determine where you fit and consider where others are coming from, you'll gain insight into yourself, family members, and friends. There is no need to stress about your starting point. Whether you are Poor, a Debtor, Dreamer, Accumulator, or Rich but Empty, don't judge; just observe. The opportunity is to create a new reality where you can stop *hoping* things will turn out great and learn to *trust* that they will.

## The Economic Choice Point: Poor

Scarcity mentality behaviors make you feel down and out poor. This is characterized by severe difficulties with cash flow management, the excuse being that there is no cash flow to manage. Living on the edge has become your way of life. If this is your category, you might feel that the people who owe you money are to blame. Perhaps you blame the government, your employer, or your family for being stuck where you are. It's a situation where misery loves company, and there is no visible way out.

I certainly know this to be true; Scarcity mentality can come from growing up in a large family where there was never enough. Or, possibly you were a single child or had one or two siblings or grew up reliant upon food stamps or public housing in a poverty-stricken community. People manage to work their way out of these circumstances but are often plagued by the fear of being poor again.

## The Economic Choice Point: Debtor

Debtors are a hybrid, crossing categories into a Scarcity mindset. They have access to credit but often run scores below 600, which draws higher interest rates. They try to get a handle on cash flow and improve their scores, but when new credit offers arrive in the mail, they can't resist, and the downward cycle repeats again.

Debtors seldom realize they create the drama themselves by overspending and never paying off all of their credit card debt. They justify borrowing from one account to pay another by saying, "I'm taking this 401k loan out because I am paying myself the interest that I am charged." That's just another way of denying financial reality. When their credit score starts moving upward, they buy the dream house or condo and furnish it all at one time, using the store's 0 percent interest for one year, without having a game plan to pay off, let's say, the $15,000 bill when the 24 percent interest rate hits them hard.

## JORDAN:
## A Debtor Seeking Financial Rebirth

Jordan was that single, sexy guy you used to see in the bar scene in your 20s. When we met, he was in his mid-30s. He appeared to be a ruggedly handsome and creative web designer. Inside, though, he was a total train wreck, emotionally and financially. He certainly seemed to have the perfect dream life, traveling extensively, wearing designer clothes, driving a vintage Ferrari, and surrounded by a bevy of beautiful girlfriends. However, his internal dialog was stuck on, "I never have enough money to pay all my bills." How could that be?

In reality, he led a very shallow life built upon a cracked foundation. What he didn't understand—and this was the impetus that brought him to see me—was why his salary was in the same range as everyone else he worked with but they seemed far less stressed about money. Once we started speaking, it became clear that he had a very common problem, one I lived through myself.

Growing up, Jordan knew there was never enough money. At age 12, he became responsible for his own expenses and clothing. When it came to financing his college education, he was also on his own. His personal philosophy was "fake it until you make it!" Unfortunately, that reasoning perpetuated his childhood reality: the poor me Scarcity story. Being "poor" and in debt, he stayed in his job, not because he loved it but because it gave him the salary to pay most of his bills and appear to be living the high life.

Over time, work seemed more like a prison sentence—until a personal crisis in his family became his catalyst for change. A beloved relative was diagnosed with a terminal illness, and Jordan saw the fragility of life "up close and personal." It was like a 2x4 cracked him over the head one last time, and it hurt enough to make him shift. Jordan knew he wanted to create a happier and healthier lifestyle.

He turned out to be an eager student, happy to embrace PACT as a roadmap toward action. He left my office after the very first visit with a realistic accounting of his debts, current cash inflows, outflows, and assets. Within weeks, he took the steps needed to come to terms with his emotions behind money. Once he figured out his true life goals and priorities, he set up a series of financial buckets to help him monetize and energize his life. PACT provided him with a clear path out of his childhood's limiting beliefs and into his own desired future.

## The Economic Choice Point: Dreamer

The dreamers among us are a blend of Scarcity and Abundance. They are pretty good at cash flow management and believe great things can happen, but are unclear as to how to get there. They may deposit matching funds into their employer's retirement plan, but if there is no matching plan, chances are they are not saving anywhere else. Back in 2008 and 2009, many dreamers stopped adding into their 401k when the market dropped because they didn't want to lose any more money. I remember asking them, "You're only putting in the match amount, about 3-5 percent, and then when the markets dropped, you decided you'd stop contributing altogether? So, you don't want to retire one day? I suggest you shift how you invest your money but do not stop contributing."

There are a lot of possibilities, but since dreamers are unsure of the roadmap, they tend to bounce around and are unlikely to pay off their credit card balances monthly. Due to challenged credit scores, they have mortgage debt at a higher rate. They can be income affluent but struggle with becoming asset affluent. Most likely, they had student loans and may feel inferior to others who come from more financially abundant families and communities. Dreamers are less likely to have a natural community of money mentors for support and guidance.

Look beyond your current group to move from dreaming to wealth manifestation. Possibly you know someone who is prudent with cash flow. Spend time with her to learn how she manages cash flow and debt. Also consider joining an association similar to SCORE, which offers business and financial support and mentoring with your finances. When I first started out, I wanted to surround myself with successful women business owners because I didn't know any growing up. I attended extremely helpful workshops, seminars, and luncheons with the Women's Business Development Center in Chicago in order to meet women who were successfully doing what I wanted to do.

## MIRANDA:
# Life as a Dreamer

People today are exhausted. We are exhausted because we are suffering in some area of our lives. Most of us are well organized in one area in our life as another one falls apart. Miranda was single, never married, in her 40s and had been working as an architect for 20 years. She had a stable job with a good income but felt undervalued and never asked for a raise. She traveled the world and had close family and friends, but yearned to have a family herself. She considered all the options, including adopting, freezing her eggs, and surrogacy. For her, motherhood was non-negotiable. She was unwilling to go through life without having children but had no clue as to how she wanted to make it happen.

Without realizing it, she was living the life of a victim—a role she played with her mother, siblings, friends, boyfriends, and employer. When these archetypes are set in our automatic response system as how we think we are supposed to act, our behavior and words continually reinforce it. When she finally had to make some kind of decision about getting pregnant, she decided to freeze her eggs.

The initial result was a complete disaster. After all of the grueling, expensive, and difficult preparations, not one egg was viable. She decided to try again. The second time around, the hormone injections made her so physically ill she had to stop. A long grieving process followed, and she was depressed for about six months. I suggested that her body's negative response meant she should try another route. I asked, "Is there another avenue you might consider?" At the time, she couldn't even think about it because she was still too upset.

Over the next year, Miranda focused on putting her financial life in order. Previously, her credit card debt hovered at around $7K. A holiday bonus arrived, and she used it to pay some of it off, but by the time the next bonus came, the debt was back up to where it had been.

For the past 10 years, her annual raises were a miniscule 2 percent. She was stuck, but always dreamed of more.

Miranda shifted her financial energy by using her next bonus to completely pay off her debt and create emergency reserves, along with allocations for vacations, a new carpet, and her retirement, breaking herself free of the debt cycle. With her finances in better order, Miranda returned to her dreams of starting a family and began the process of private adoption. She was deep into the process when the birth mother opted to keep the child. Miranda was understandably devastated, and her debts returned almost immediately. Unfortunately, this is a common pattern.

Miranda became comfortable living with that level of debt and decided to become a foster parent. No one she knew had done this before, but she felt she was being called to do it and was willing to let go of anything that stood in her way. She loved the idea of helping a child have a better chance in life, providing the comfort of a home for someone in need.

She fostered a few different children, closely watched her budget, and began dating again. The final empowering moment came when she admitted to herself that her employer didn't value her work. As she accepted that reality, she updated her resume and began applying for new jobs. Allowing herself to dream of a better position, she soon landed a new job at $30K more per year.

Throughout this process, Miranda redefined her idea of a family, improved her professional life and financial status, and lost weight. She turned her life around on every level, facing and dealing with past emotions to become her true self, no longer living the life of a victim. Now she is free to continue dreaming for the future from a sound financial platform. I love when that happens. It is why I do what I do!

## The Economic Choice Point: Accumulator

Accumulators move in and out of financial Scarcity and Abundance and tend to be on the high side of the Hybrid mentality, spending more time on the Abundance side. They often have "good debt," such as mortgages, car loans, or a student loan at competitive rates. Most of the time, they live within their means. Accumulators are typically saving not only in their retirement plans at work, but also on their own. They likely have some emergency reserve in a savings account, but not necessarily enough. They have convinced themselves that most of their debt is good and are unaware that those debts are weighing them down. Accumulators tend to pay off their credit cards monthly, but occasionally overspend before getting back on track.

## LISA:
## Accumulator in Action

Lisa was a typical accumulator, age 35, with all the vigor and vitality needed to change the world. She was just beginning to accept her financial reality and dig in to create a new one. Lisa took on debt to finance her future, but paid off her undergraduate student loans by age 30. She cringed at the thought of carrying revolving credit card debt and paid it all off within 45-60 days. She never married. She adored her nieces and nephews and started college fund savings accounts for each of them. She began planning for retirement in her mid-20s by contributing to her employer's matched plan, and that money compounded.

Zoning in on what retirement would be like for her, she planned to retire around age 65, but knew she could comfortably do so earlier. Retirement is not only about no longer going to work—it is also about redesigning your life. The downside was Lisa's tax liability. Too much of her money went towards paying taxes, which required attention from a tax specialist each year. Her income in her 30s was at $110,000, with assets of over $130K, which were growing nicely. By the time she was 45, her net worth, which is assets minus debts, would be over $1M.

Lisa lived the life she chose by designating more of her income into savings. Younger accumulators like to think about settling down by purchasing a home, with or without a partner, while older ones have already settled down. Lisa was financially stable on her own and was able to financially stand on her own two feet now, as she would also be able to do later on.

## The Economic Choice Point: Rich but Empty

People who are Rich but Empty may be financially abundant but feel their life lacks meaning and purpose. For them, it's not really about money or wealth accumulation any more. This group has the money. If you feel Rich but Empty, you may possibly be detached from your soul's needs. It's quite likely you carry little or no debt and have a high quality of life, but you may have thought that once you reached this point, everything would be spectacular.

Money has definitely helped, but your heart's desire is missing and your soul is *screaming* at you to pay attention. Your body and mind will be unsettled until you soothe your soul, energize your life, and figure out your heart's desire. It's time to be authentic. If you follow PACT and are introspective and take action, you will become truly wealthy in all aspects of your life.

## PATTY:
## Rich but No Longer Empty

Here's a story about real wealth and living in abundant authenticity. Patty used PACT to zone in on her desired future.

Picturing her life set her up for success. She climbed her way through the ranks from one of the lowest rungs on the ladder. A single mom with seven children and working as a waitress, she jumped at a small business opportunity that came her way. She always wanted to be her own boss, create a high quality of life, and provide income so that her children would not struggle financially and would learn how to manage and value money.

She grew her business gradually, creating financial security, and invested wisely throughout the years. Once her children were all grown up and educated, she paid off her primary residence along with a vacation home. For her business, she hired a president while remaining CEO. She currently has more than 50 employees who enjoy being part of this thriving business. Patty has made it.

When we spoke most recently, she said an inexplicable sadness had come over her, as if she were having some kind of spiritual awakening. She found herself an empty nester, happily remarried, and a wildly successful business owner, but something was missing. As we talked, I kept asking, "Do you have the space in your life to pursue something else?" She didn't, so she hired a new president who could take over the reins of the day-to-day business operations. Patty was now ready to follow her calling.

Connecting with her soul, she became clear on her strongest gifts. Patty wanted to inspire single moms to break out of cycles of generational poverty. She challenged them to become more aware of their own needs and those of their communities. She knew from experience how to rise up from the trenches and make something of herself and wanted to teach other women to do the same.

She raised funds to benefit children of single-parent households by educating their parents. This calling, and her generosity towards others, has brought her even more money, publicity, business, and satisfaction than she ever imagined. Using PACT, she chose to meditate and practice yoga, ultimately finding a holistic life coach.

Patty realizes now that she was Rich but Empty and has discovered a way to energetically raise her internal sense of self by serving others.

## MONEY ENERGIZING TIME:
# How to Accept Your True Self

**ME TIME**   Create a list of five people you admire most, along with the top-five attributes or traits they have. Then make a list of the people in your life who drive you crazy and include their most difficult characteristics. Take a good look at these two lists because *you have just described yourself!*

The good, the bad, and the ugly are all, in some way, a reflection of your personality. These people are in your life because you resonate with them. The secret to a more balanced and authentic life is to spend more time interacting and speaking with people you admire and choose to emulate. At the same time, gradually phase out time spent with people who bring you down and reinforce your feeling of being completely depleted.

## MICHAEL:
# Finding Joy in Your Authenticity

When my friend, Michael, and I were in our late 20s, he lived his life day by day, not terribly enthusiastic about it. He had watched all of his friends leave for college while he stayed home to work in a trade he did not love, and he always regretted it. Michael's Italian immigrant parents worked odd jobs their entire lives and kept telling him how much they would have loved having a trade like his at his age. To them, Michael had hit the lottery, but Michael was not satisfied.

I suggested that he make a wish list and start detaching from what he thought he was supposed to do, or should do, and move to what he dreamt of doing. Within minutes, this list included lots of great things: to attend a Notre Dame football game, go to a professional basketball game, leave town on his vacation days, visit Europe, travel to a major league baseball stadium outside Chicago, go to a Chicago Bears game, and much more. It was interesting to me that everything on his list seemed pretty easy to do, but to him they were monumental tasks. He never imagined he could reach out and grab each and every one of his dreams. At the time, I had no clue as to why he wouldn't just go buy football tickets or other things he wanted.

His second layer was his parents' frugality. They ingrained in him to never waste money. You didn't spend unless you had enough in the bank, but there was never enough. I decided to take him to a Chicago Bulls basketball game. That was the start of his new beginning. He enjoyed it so much that it triggered something in him that led to a totally different future. Over the next two years, Michael fulfilled each of his desires. When his first list was completed, he made a second one, adding and tackling bigger and more challenging dreams. This exercise helped him build his muscles. He realized how much he loved sports.

When a friend asked him to help coach grade-school football, Michael added that to his list. He became aware of the infinite possibilities in this world, even to the point of changing his career. Five years after making the first list, Michael went back to college to become a physical therapist. The moral to this story is to see you for the real you, not where you've been pigeon-holed.

Awaken to your authenticity. It's about loving yourself enough to give yourself permission to go for it. Accept your reality and express gratitude for all the experiences you've had in life thus far, because you would not be where you are without them. PACT guides you to be in sync with your cash flow, not spending money you don't have, so you can live in the present moment.

JULIE'S GEMS:
# Love the One You Are With

Coming to terms with my own reality and uncovering my own authentic self was definitely an adventure. I could either hate that I am a *big* woman or choose to love every ounce of me. It's the body I was given, and I am happier loving it rather than fighting it. I had unresolved emotions stuck inside my fat cells. I tried a detox to clear my system. It made me extremely sad. All the years of being ridiculed for being fat were ready to come up and out. The release of those toxins and emotions caused an amazing transformation in my physical body and created space in my heart and mind to expand my spirit.

At that time, I remember a friend asking me if I was changing religions when I started to meditate. At its core, meditation is about being open to listening. Some people like to meditate to music, while others like to have someone guide them, and still others use a mantra or chanting technique. When I meditate, I hear my own spirit in ways I never have before. The more I learned about my spirit, the more self-nurturing I became. Today, I attract more loving and successful people to me than ever before, along with great financial and personal abundance. This has become my new reality, and I have every confidence it will happen for you, too, once you seek out your authentic self.

Why do we choose not to learn more about ourselves? We have deep-seated fears of becoming our true selves because then we might no longer identify with the world we've created. It feels safer to stay stuck in a life that is familiar. We have been trained not to be selfish, but there is a huge difference between being self-nurturing and being selfish. You must take care of you first. When you do, you'll be happier and do all the things you never thought you could. When you are clear about who you are and live it every day, stress disappears. Coming from a place of being your own authority exudes confidence and attracts others because they want what you've got. You are raising your energetic vibration to bring more love, money, and opportunities into your world.

## Energy Work and Authenticity

Attending one of Deepak Chopra's symposiums, I heard scientists and researchers from around the world speak on every topic imaginable related to the mind, body, and spirit. Both Stuart Hameroff, MD, and Candace Pert, PhD, stated that 95 percent of our responses to the physical world come from our subconscious. That intrigued me because I have found, in working with clients and money, so much of our financial framework is created subconsciously, without our awareness, through pattern imprinting as we grew up. We think we arrive at adulthood knowing everything we need; instead, we lack the true experience of making our own choices and decisions.

Habits and attitudes you just can't shake off most likely reside in your subconscious. These are typically limiting beliefs that need to be worked out. One client grew up being told she was fragile and had to be careful because of her health. She experienced a series of rather severe illnesses as a young child; however, they were cured. She was well, but her parents could not let go of their concerns and continued limiting her activities. Their fears affected her education, her job choices, and just about every decision she ever made in her life.

One day, she was in therapy for an issue with one of her children and experienced her own "aha!" moment. "It was a revelation, like watching myself in an old family movie," she remembered. "I walked out of that office ready to claim my life, my finances, my resources, and everything around me. This is my life, not my parents' and not my children's, nor my husband's. I am determined to live the rest of my days, loving all of them but listening to myself as my own guide in my own way." She learned what I truly believe: our intuition is the only true guide to life.

## MONEY ENERGIZING TIME:
## Looking at Your Earliest Adult Influences

**ME TIME**    This is an exercise designed to illustrate how you can accept reality and awaken authenticity. We all have limiting beliefs that play a role in how we act each day. Many times we don't recognize our beliefs are impacting our daily decisions. The experiences you have had thus far have molded how you act today. If something was painful for you in the past, you might go out of your way to avoid anything similar to it. This becomes more obvious when you look at the economic conditions you've been subjected to. These could be macro-level issues, like the economy at large, or more micro-level concerns that are personal. Respond to the following questions to see how your past has really affected the decisions you make today:

- ♥ What was the state of the economy when you were ages 18-25, just as you launched yourself as an adult?
- ♥ Were jobs plentiful when you got out of school and started your career?
- ♥ Did you come from a family who provided funds for college, or did you come out of school with loads of debt?
- ♥ Did you have a great support system—physically, financially, and emotionally—to be exactly who you

were drawn to be? Or were you told you were not enough or weren't the right version?

- ♥ Besides student loan debt, how were your other debt levels from car, credit cards, house, or condo when you were mid-career?
- ♥ Where do those debts stand now?
- ♥ Did you regret your choice of degree?
- ♥ Did you succumb to what you "should have" gotten your degree in, or did you study exactly what you actually desired?
- ♥ What else was going on in your world, on a macro or micro level, that impacted your decision-making process as a young adult?

Carefully consider each of your responses. Are you still making decisions today because you "should" do something or because you really want to? Are you only choosing the financially prudent things while avoiding living in the present moment? Do you feel guilty if you choose something your heart desires? Take a thoughtful look at how your younger years have impacted you today. Now choose. Tell yourself, *I'm going to live a guilt-free life.*

Choose to live a life rooted in heart-based decisions. Ask yourself if the things you are choosing now are going to create the future you desire. Is this what you want to create, moving forward in your life? If you're not sure, how is your body responding right now? Is your body tightening up or feeling anxious? Your body is one friend you can always count on to tell you the truth. As you can see, it all boils down to your choices. That's what creates everything in your world. Now choose wisely.

The last story for this chapter is about a woman who ultimately chose to put herself first and was much better off because of it.

## SUZANNE:
# Moving Forward into a Truly Authentic Life

I met Suzanne, a woman in her early 50s, two years into her fight for a divorce, struggling with setting her own boundaries and living life by her own rules. Throughout her 20-year marriage, her husband, a successful business owner, dictated every facet of their lives. With the youngest child in high school, she decided it was time to end the strained marriage. She decided to give herself freedom and to give the children she loved one healthy, wonderful parent. She had no control over the other one.

She had become increasingly disenfranchised by the dynamics of her marriage, not only financially but also emotionally. She begged for money to pay the household bills and for her own personal needs because her husband held money over her as part of his power play against her. She raised their children by herself because he was always working, but as they grew up, he started manipulating them with money also. The more Suzanne tried setting boundaries, the more he enticed the children with gifts and money while making Suzanne out to be the villain.

When we met, she was still trying to stay afloat by paying the household bills from her investments because he had cut off her cash flow. I asked, "Why don't you just stop paying the bills?" I knew this would force the sale of the house. She responded that would be too hard for her. She would have to walk away from the home in which she raised her family. She wanted to keep her youngest son in the high school he attended. Then her son decided to move in with his father and change schools. As he moved out, she realized there was no compelling reason to stay in the house.

Then came the final straw: she discovered her husband had hacked into her computer and saw everything she was doing. She felt violated enough to stand firm with her personal boundaries and was angry and strong enough to stop paying the household bills and move out. The house became her ex-husband's problem.

While that scenario played out, we kept working through the PACT process to allow her to picture the life of her dreams. So far, her life had not turned out the way she had hoped, as her husband and children had also turned on her. My advice was to branch out and create the life she wanted before any more time passed. She heard my words, accepted where she was in life, and reassessed her own wants by tuning in to her own authenticity. The PACT questionnaires showed her that she had choices, and she began dreaming of a new life. She hated Chicago winters, so she decided to move to Florida. She used a portion of her divorce settlement to purchase a small home there.

Suzanne also decided to stop the vicious fight for her half of the marriage assets and to take another approach. We came up with the amount of money she could live on monthly, which was very different compared to her previous, more lavish married life. We proposed to the attorneys that she be given an investible lump sum to produce the $6,000 per month income to support the lifestyle she chose for the rest of her life. The attorneys thought she was crazy for walking away from the additional millions she might see if she kept fighting, but this solution provided her with peace of mind. No amount of money was worth continuing the battle. She had spent too many years caught in this power struggle and was ready to move on.

A few years later, Suzanne was loving life and flourishing. Her husband kept pulling power plays on their children, and they eventually distanced themselves from their father. Suzanne is thrilled to have her grown children back in tune with her. Suzanne's story illustrates that sometimes we really do need to lead by example. It was extremely difficult for her to walk away from her children, but she trusted it would all work out. She chose self-love and personal peace over a lifetime of continued struggles. That is the power PACT delivers.

All of these personal stories, including my own, highlight the importance of finding our authentic selves and accepting our reality; this also includes the choices we will make in our future. The next chapter, the "C" in PACT is for "Choosing to Change," builds upon the critical choices leading to transformation.

## Financial Meditation

*I am enough. I was created with everything I need to live a full, exciting, and adventurous life. My mind, body, and soul support my being; at the same time, money supports my well-being, dreams, goals, and aspirations. Together, this dynamic duo works as one whole, giving me a fulfilled, organic life. I accept, celebrate, and am grateful for who I am, where I am, and where I am going.*

# CHAPTER 6

# C: CHOOSING TO CHANGE

---

*Too many people spend money they haven't earned, to buy
things they don't want, to impress people that they don't like.*
**~WILL ROGERS**

---

At six years old, I thought I'd won the lottery. I deposited my first check for delivering newspapers. It was my one giant step toward leaving poverty behind. Even at that young age, I realized that money provided choices in life. My mother always said, "Sometimes you just have to make do with what you have," and we always did. We made everything stretch: money, clothes, food, toys. The gifts we gave out at Christmas were recycled, decorated oatmeal containers filled with homemade cookies for our aunts and uncles. It felt good to give Christmas gifts from the heart, but as I got older, I couldn't help dreaming about living a different life—which certainly has come true.

Physically, as human beings, we are comprised of energy, a mass of constantly traveling atoms and molecules. Quantum physics teaches us that positive energy, thoughts, words, and feelings attract positive events, circumstances, and money. Research scientists are proving this is based on actual facts, facts we can build on to propel us to who, what, and where we want to be.

There are some excellent resources to help you learn more. Dr. Joe Dispenza's book *Breaking the Habit of Being Yourself* combines quantum physics, neuroscience, brain chemistry, biology, and genetics to explain how all human beings create the reality they each choose. His work reinforces what my clients and I, and now you, too, are modeling and living. It begins with identifying a clear vision of your intentions by changing your choices.

## Intention as a Power Tool

Your intentions, the trigger for change, are the most powerful and crucial tool in wealth building. This is a spiritual process that opens doors to infinite possibilities. Universal energies interact, combine, and assist, molecule by molecule, atom by atom, to manifest your plans. Professional athletes mentally practice their golf swings, free throws, or triple axel jumps for years before stepping foot on the fairway, basketball court, or skating rink.

Former world champion gymnast and human potential coach Dan Millman tells his story in *Way of the Peaceful Warrior* of how he broke free of debilitating performance pressure by living in the moment in alignment with his heart. His story is riveting as he intimately describes how there can be no forward motion in our lives without very clear passion, commitment, and intent. Rather than staying broken in body and spirit following a severe injury, he chose to focus all efforts on going for Olympic gold. As part of his daily routine, he shifted his customized workouts based on his physical stamina.

Healing with each step moved him closer to reaching his goal, which is exactly what we are doing with PACT. When clear and deliberate intent is used, in combination with taking action toward our goals, we can reach every goal. This is especially true with money. You have the power to change your current financial situation simply by turning your heart's desires and dreams into intentions. This chapter will show you how.

But first, prepare yourself by adjusting your self-talk. Be loving and considerate of your feelings and needs. Eliminate the word "hate" from your vocabulary. My grandfather always said, "Hate is a harsh word." I agree. Speaking in "hateful" terms shuts you off from attempting any change because it doesn't leave any room for understanding the problem. The same reasoning applies to angry explosions that emit low-energetic vibrations, which make it impossible to tap into the quantum field and improve your situation.

By all means, be frustrated and challenged and express your emotions, energetically speaking. Think about this. Visualize being hooked up to a machine measuring the mega Hz you are vibrating at; it would show you that being frustrated measures at a much higher rate than being angry. You have the opportunity to identify the aspects of your life that are frustrating you and creatively figure out a way to approach them differently.

## MONEY ENERGIZING TIME:
## Choosing to Change

**ME TIME**   The first step is to claim what you want and then take small steps each day towards achieving gold. Make a list of the choices you want to make in your life, starting now. You are the designer of your future. What positive financial choices will you make? What unhealthy financial choices will you leave behind?

## Cleansing Exercise

Think of cleansing away everything you dislike about your current situation as cleaning out the refrigerator—removing the old and making room for the new. Close your eyes and let your mind explore the possibilities of releasing each of these items. Then complete "I choose to _____," with your newly chosen behaviors. Here are a few suggestions:

- ♥ I choose to live within my means.
- ♥ I choose to face my current financial reality.
- ♥ I choose work that is in alignment with my soul.
- ♥ I choose to nurture treasured relationships with my family.

Or simply state your intent:

- ♥ I choose to save $100 a month for six months.
- ♥ I choose to have a positive relationship with money.
- ♥ I choose to have wealth in Abundance.
- ♥ I choose to proactively reduce my debt balances.
- ♥ I choose to log my health progress on "My Fitness Pal" daily to become more aware of my nutritional choices.
- ♥ I choose to love myself enough to lose excess weight.
- ♥ I choose to wear my FitBit daily and hit 10,000 steps per day.
- ♥ I choose to update my resume and share it with the world.

The possibilities are endless because they are *yours*. We live in a quantum field of infinite opportunities. Carefully read through your lists, rewriting statements on sticky notes and plastering them all over your home as constant reminders of how you choose to live. Repeat them throughout your day with the assumption that they have already happened. It won't be long before these conscious choices become your "clear intent," creating new behaviors and a new reality.

## Reaping What You Sow

Time and time again, I meet clients who hate their boss, the company, and their job. Interestingly enough, these same individuals do not receive raises, bonuses, or promotions. Why do they stay? They stay because they cannot afford to move on; they need the money. The 2008 and 2009 recession hit hard, and many people saw their salaries slashed by as much as 25 percent. Amidst all of this financial chaos, in December 2008, my client Robert received a windfall. "Julie, you're not going to believe this. I received a $30,000 bonus," he told me.

Two years earlier, he traded in a sedentary and routine job he disliked for his dream job. He envisioned himself being in charge of an advertising agency's creative department where his decisions directly impacted the business at large, and that is exactly what he landed. Creative freedom, extensive travel, and a 20 percent salary increase made him very happy.

On the flipside, in 2010, I was teaching a seminar on how to embrace your career to the fullest. A 50-ish woman kept interrupting me. The name on her badge said "Debbie," and her negative comments were all about how employers don't care about their workers any more. She shared her story of devoting her life to the company for 25 years. In 2009, when they downsized, she was one of 484 people laid off. Her anger and negativity permeated the room. I decided to use her as an example by asking her to share her work history with us.

It turned out that a family friend, who knew the owner of the company, helped Debbie secure the high-paying job right out of high school. As the years went by, she admitted that she lost her passion for the work. Promotions passed her by, and her anger at being unappreciated fueled her apathy. When the recession hit in 2008, she was thankful she had a job, but by then, her anger, which in actuality was extreme sadness, was evident in *all* of her actions, behavior, and words.

Debbie had become a toxic presence at work. Instead of taking responsibility, she played the role of the victim, believing she hadn't received what she was entitled to. She blamed everyone else for her problems. It had been clear for years that she needed to make a change, but she did not listen. She chose instead to stay with the familiar, in her comfort zone, rather than venturing into something that would feed her soul. Occasionally, when she was aware of the messages she received, she lacked the courage to change.

I asked her if she would be willing to become more open to the possibility of something better out there for her, but she didn't return after the lunch break. She was still unwilling to change. By refusing to take this necessary step, Debbie's negativity would continue to tie her down to her miserable situation.

## Accepting Responsibility

This exercise will explore your behavioral patterns. Write down your responses in your notebook to the following questions.

- ♥ How do you get what you want?
- ♥ Do you take responsibility for your mistakes and devise a solution to rectify the situation, or do you frequently play the victim to gain sympathy and manipulate others to let you have your way?
- ♥ How is that working for you?
- ♥ Do you rush into situations in a panic for fear of coming in second?
- ♥ Do you think objectively? If not, how do you think that could change things?
- ♥ Do you use your creativity to brainstorm a variety of paths to achieve your goals and select the most meaningful one for you? If not, why not?

♥ What's keeping you stuck in this paralyzed position, and are you willing to move forward?

Think about a recent success, achievement, or acquisition.

♥ How did you get it?
♥ What energy did you use in the process?

Consider the last time you bought a car or your last big purchase or decision.

♥ What steps did you take to attain it?
♥ What emotions or behaviors did you use?
♥ Did you set a budget for yourself, or did you sweet talk your partner or parents into providing the funds?
♥ Did you compare competitive dealerships?
♥ What was your demeanor with salespeople?
♥ Were you charming, businesslike, or demanding?
♥ Did you research which car was right for you and base your planned cash outflow on that car loan?
♥ Did you drive all over town for a week to find the ideal car, or did the whole transaction occur in 10 minutes?

When our behavior patterns continually create drama and negative consequences, they distract us from achieving our goals. Your behavior may be wreaking havoc on your relationships with others and yourself.

Read over your narrative. Can you see yourself following one or more specific behaviors when you try to get what you want? Are the behaviors healthy or harmful? Are they Scarcity or Abundance actions? Don't over think this. Simply ask yourself, *What are my habitual patterns?* This is not about good or bad, right or wrong. It's just something for you to recognize and think about, without self-judgment.

## Knowing When to Consult with Experts

Depending on your habits, choices, and purchasing decisions, I'd likely steer you in the direction of experts in three categories. I call them Normal, Tweeners, and Esoteric experts. These are professionals with special knowledge and techniques who can assist you in your financial, work, personal, family, and spiritual life.

The first category are those resources I consider "Normal" options in the traditional financial world. These are socially acceptable and widely used professionals to help you on your journey. Some people prefer to use certified public accountants (CPAs), while others are comfortable with certified tax preparers, bookkeepers, or TurboTax software. You might also consult with business attorneys, estate planning attorneys, employee benefit specialists, mortgage brokers, qualified retirement planning specialists, and real estate brokers. All of these professionals are trained to assist you with specific financial areas. No matter how well you know your advisor, make sure you always ask questions. Put your own desires first and maintain your own personal power. Your relationship with your financial planner should be taken as seriously as any other partnership you enter into.

Listen to the experts. Take into account what they say while consulting your own feelings and thoughts on the matter. Both parties need to understand the "why" behind what you are doing. Check to see if what they recommend fits your intentions for what you want to create, then implement what's right for you—not what constitutes a knee-jerk reaction or a quick fix.

"Tweeners" are experts who can assist you in a variety of non-financial areas of your life that indirectly affect your money on a conscious level. These include career coaches, recruiting firms, family or marital therapists, business valuation experts, nutritionists, and personal trainers. These professionals assist in processing your emotions to avoid their blocking your progress. They may directly affect your finances, but the areas they counsel you in generally impact your finances in harder-to-see ways.

Emotions are excess energy in our bodies. If we deny our feelings, they will appear in the form of illness or financial chaos. Your buried emotions will rise up again as soon as you manage to get your money in order. If you are aware that you need to improve your eating habits or strengthen your workout regimen, connect with the resources to best address your underlying issues. Believe me, changes in areas of your life "outside" of your finances will bolster your bank balance.

"Esoteric" professionals can assist you in clearing subconscious areas that could be keeping you from moving forward. These experts work in "energy psychology" and include Psych-K, Holographic Re-patterning, hypnotherapy, Neuro Emotional Technique (NET), Emotional Freedom Technique (EFT), and Thought Field Therapy (TFT). As a financial planner, I have developed strategic alliances with professional healers who assist clients in overcoming blocks and moving out of their own way. If you find yourself repeating behavioral patterns over and over again and you choose to stop but cannot, this is a sign that you might need some additional help.

## MONEY ENERGIZING TIME:
### Travel Across the Bridge

**ME TIME**    By this point in the book, you have pictured what you want in your ideal world, accepted your reality, and become attuned to your authentic self. This is the moment in your PACT journey where you need to accept right where you are and choose to see yourself crossing the bridge to where you want to go. Do not worry about how; just put one foot in front of the other and walk.

Soon enough, you'll be running faster than you had ever imagined toward your new financial future.

Don't be afraid to feel the emotions as they come up so that you can begin to let them go. Tell yourself, *I'm going to be fine*, and keep repeating the phrase as you walk toward your future. This visualization is powerful because you have now made a conscious choice to move forward toward your new goals. It signals the Universe that you are prepared for the change. Congratulations!

## The Beautiful Power of Choice

I truly believe that life is about choices. The life you live is an amalgamation of these choices. Right now, today, you can consciously choose what your future is going to be. Show me what a person is doing right this moment, and I will tell you what his or her financial future looks like. People often underestimate the power of the next 24 hours. I can anticipate your objections: "Julie, that's all good and fine, but just choosing to create wealth isn't going to pay off the $14,000 balance on my Visa bill or send my children to college. It won't allow me to work fewer hours at my job or spend more time with my grandchildren." Oh, yes it will, because once you choose to change and claim your personal power, your financial life will never again be the same. Your intentions are the keys to building wealth. Without them, you're just a sitting duck. By setting intentions and applying practical actions to those goals, you will begin to see positive results. Energy flows where energy goes!

## Is There Ever *Enough*?

What happens when we suffer from a lack of "enough" money? It has nothing to do with your level of income, but rather your lifestyle choices and expenses. If you lack the income to sustain your lifestyle, decide what you are willing to give up. The less you are willing to adjust, the longer it will take to align your lifestyle with your desired cash flow. Having trouble making ends meet is most often dependent upon past accumulated debts. Committing future income to pay down debt can take a very long time.

This is why so many of us stay in jobs we dislike—because we are supporting past choices. The average working American carries mortgage, car, credit card, and/or student loan debt. Today student loans must be signed by both the students and parents, putting many adults into the position of paying off their own loans and then being faced with the economic reality of education in this country—paying off their children's debts.

PACT can help in all of these areas. You can clean up your financial past, while still living in the present moment and simultaneously planning for the future. The time to zone in on your personal financial priorities is ideally before incurring debt, not after. Instead of impulsively buying a new car, consider a game plan that does not include incurring debt. You can still buy the car you need. Mark and Annie's story illustrates an alternative way to make choices when faced with tough decisions.

## Does Life Just Happen?

Mark and Annie, in their 30s, struggled with how to buy a house and larger family car without creating a financial upheaval. They had a pattern of racking up credit card debt, paying it down, and then encountering crises that *made them* build it back up. When their hot water heater broke, their emergency reserves had been used the month before to repair the front porch steps. Consequently, the new hot water heater went on their credit card.

Both Mark and Annie maintained the attitude that "life happens." But did that attitude lead them to make some unwise choices along the way? They paid for their wedding with borrowed money—it didn't "just happen." They assumed their wedding gifts would pay off what they spent, but, of course, that was not the case. Rarely do wedding gifts come anywhere near to meeting wedding expenses.

Their marital union began in debt, and that became the norm for their relationship. They rented housing for a few years until baby number two was on the way. Annie wanted to own a typical American home with a white picket fence. Mark suggested using their 401k and do a 401k loan for the down payment, creating more cash flow pressure. Because their pattern was an unhealthy one, things that kept coming up with the new house, like the sump pump backing up and flooding the kitchen, increased their credit card debt.

Then came another surprise: baby number three. Ouch! Mark and Annie had no plans for how to manage their cash flow. When they came to me, they could not see a way out of their insane financial drama without help. They wanted to be positive role models for their children and were committed to paying off all debts. They had one paramount worry: their second mortgage had a variable interest that was rising rapidly. For the first time in their financial lives, they decided to tackle the issue head on. We focused on moving as much of the credit card debt as possible into zero percent interest accounts. They put the debt payments on autopilot, easily doable with online banking payments, to end payment negotiations when "life happened."

My next suggestion was to stop using credit cards. Without that fallback system, clients become far more frugal and creative, finding innovative solutions to attain what they need without creating more debt. Separating *need* from *want* is important. For example, Mark and Annie really wanted a bigger car. I asked if it was a *want* or a *need*. They initially said, "It's a need." But when I asked if they could squeak by for a year or two with their current car, they admitted they could.

We then discussed what else they needed to shift. I recommended that they take what they would have been spending on a monthly new car payment and automatically put that amount into a separate savings account designated as the "new car fund." By keeping this account separate, it also provided focused, positive feedback. They were moving closer to achieving their goal, making their tight squeeze in the little car more tolerable. Once the account was for the "new car" and only to be spent on that goal, they were not tempted to negotiate their intention away. They chose to not create a car payment, instead creating a new car savings account.

I understand this is not the easiest or most popular route to take, but it got them out of trouble, and it can do the same for you. As I've continually illustrated, your financial future depends on how badly you really want to change. Saving $250 per month for two years amounts to $6,000. You can buy a used car for that sum. Depending upon your priorities, it might take longer than two years. There might be other options to consider; it might become the down payment.

Another couple I counseled used this exact approach to buy a Hyundai that cost $13,000. With a substantial down payment, the monthly payment came to $150. Before the purchase, they were saving $250 per month to their "new car" savings account. After the purchase, we allocated the monthly outlay of $150 to the loan payment and opened a "next car" account with $100 automatically deposited each month. In this way, they were able to become their own bank over time. This process shifts your financial energy away from being a victim of circumstances and moves you toward being empowered by your new financial reality.

Mark and Annie also needed a fund for unexpected household costs. A "household maintenance" account was set up with an automatic $50 deposit each month. This approach allows people to live more in the present moment and stop the never-ending debt cycle. Other financial professionals tell you to only pay down the debt if you're paying high interest on it. I disagree. If you put all your extra money to debt payoff, the debt will become a never-ending-battle. The goal is to get your debt interest rate as low as possible while changing behaviors that disrupt your debt cycle. My advice is to shift your financial energy from being unable to make ends meet to easily meeting the financial means you have chosen to live by. Then you truly own your personal financial power.

Next, we will explore healing exercises that will help you avoid spending hangovers. The first one deals with wants vs. needs, and the second one shows you how to set up savings accounts that really work.

## MONEY ENERGIZING TIME:
## Is That a Want or a Need?

**ME TIME**    In today's society, there are many things we believe we *must* have. We've confused ourselves that they are actually needs, but they really are wants, not needs. We're confused because we really do want everything, and we have found emotional satisfaction by getting all those wants—whether they are material things or new experiences. Are you confused about your needs vs. your wants? This exercise will help you sort it out. Take a few minutes to look at the list below. Determine which of these items are *wants* and which are *needs*.

- ♥ Cable TV
- ♥ Car payments
- ♥ Eating out
- ♥ Holiday spending
- ♥ Paying for kids' college costs
- ♥ New clothes

If you said anything on the above list is a need, you are not on the path to financial success. Everything on the above list is a *want*. Your reaction might be, "What are you talking about? Where in the world does *want* come into play?" I hear this all the time. Yes, you need clothes; however, you don't need to go into credit card debt to buy them. Designate a certain percentage from every paycheck to build a "shopping for clothes" savings account. When the money is gone, shopping stops.

Many of us want to spend freely, but we don't have the unlimited income to support it. With every slide of the credit card, you choose debt and opt for wants over needs. You can have what you want, but those purchases should be in alignment with what your income can support.

Cable TV with movie channels is a want, not a need. One client insisted that it was a need since he purchased a bundled package covering a landline, cable, and Internet. He insisted, "That's the way it came, all together." But he did not have to purchase the package for well over $100 each month. He had a cell phone and needed Internet service, which he could have purchased at less than half the price of the bundle. This is also true for holiday spending, paying for your child's college education, eating out, and having car payments. These are all lifestyle choices. They are *not* needs.

My clients, Jenna and Jack, were distressed when they admitted, "We cannot pay for our son's college." Their friends and family were appalled, but their reasoning was sound. "We're behind in our own retirement planning. The government will lend him money to go to college, but they will not lend us money to retire, hence our decision." Of course, it would be great to assist your children and pay for their college, but you do have watch out that their education will not limit your own life. If you haven't already done so, I suggest creating a collaborative financial model that is healthy for you and your family. You cannot take care of those you love if you do not take care of yourself.

## MONEY ENERGIZING TIME:
# Naming Your Savings Accounts

**ME TIME**   This exercise is to help you raise your energetic vibration for strategic saving by stressing the importance of different online accounts for various purposes. Obviously, it makes sense to open the account with the highest interest rate, but that is not the only objective. You certainly want a competitive interest rate and to clearly identify your financial intention. We identify with account names, not numbers. For example, I maintain five different accounts for the most important things for me and my family: emergency reserves, vacation fund, real estate taxes, private high school fund, and a self-nurturing fund. Think about and feel the accounts *you* need to open for what purpose.

I have fun with my savings accounts, and I hope you will too. If you want a vacation fund, don't just call it "vacation." Be specific. Call it your "Italy fund." Once I had an account that was called my "boat fund" because I really wanted to buy a boat. Once I realized I wanted a sailboat, I renamed it "sailboat fund." When I drilled down and figured out I wanted a 34-foot Beneteau sailboat, guess what? Yep, I renamed it the "34-foot Beneteau fund." The more specific you can be about your intention, the more likely you are to manifest it.

Every year, I do something special to feed my soul. Last year, I attended Ayurveda health classes. Having money set aside to nurture myself reinforces that the time

is well-deserved, and I can enjoy it without guilt because
it is prepaid.

 ## MONEY ENERGIZING TIME:
### Decision Time

**ME TIME**   "Whatever you are not changing, you are choosing,"
says blogger and author Laurie Buchannan. Up to this
point, you have been working with how much money you
have or the income you are producing. But it doesn't have
to stay like this forever. You can choose to change that
now. Feel it, know it, *do it.*

We talked about patterns, and this is another chance
to identify yours. Do you want to keep repeating old
habits that are not working for you, or do you want relief?
The first reality check is to recognize what you are doing
and decide to adjust. In chapter 5 when you summarized
your current financials, you began by simply opening up
the envelopes with bills in them. With that choice, you
moved through the avoidance stage and into acceptance.
You are now ready to move on to making some important
new choices.

When you receive your next pay raise, don't just
allocate 100 percent of the extra money to more spending.
Automatically use 30-50 percent of your newfound
wealth, after deducting income taxes, to fund your desired
future and to avert more credit card debt. Think of this
as losing weight. You have to reduce the calories you
eat daily until the excess fat disappears. Once you are at
your ideal weight, you can gradually increase your caloric
intake. Since you lived for so long consuming extra
calories—or incurring extra debt—at some point you

have to scale back to find a balance. Part of this process is to acknowledge the patterns that are currently dictating your life and decide what path you will *choose*.

When you created your list in chapter 5, you acknowledged that your debt, cash flow, and assets were all of your own making. You're now aware that your wealth must be built from the inside out. Your soul's desire is one thing, but if your actions do not support it, you will not achieve sustainable wealth. The two need to move in unison, not detract from one another.

Over the years, while teaching workshops, I often hear, "If I just declare bankruptcy, then I can start all over." Sorry to rain on your parade, but it's not that easy. Chances are, you would make the same mistakes all over again because you haven't internalized your reality or built up your financial muscles. Bankruptcy also has lots of terrible repercussions. It is not a sustainable remedy and should be avoided if at all possible.

## Understanding Cash Flow

Cash is king! It is a very different experience to slide a credit card to pay for a purchase compared to handing over a $100 bill. There is an emotional and physical attachment to cash versus credit. When we hand over a $100 bill, we internalize what we are spending, but there's a total disconnect when paying with credit or debit. Purchasing online is even easier; a few clicks of the mouse and money is spent that does not register until the bill arrives.

I encourage everyone to use cash. For clients with cash flow issues, I ask them to use only cash for every purchase for two solid months. The results are amazing. Spending levels are reduced on average by 10-30 percent. This happens because we make more conscious spending choices when giving up part of the cash we have visibly available. We might need it.

According to my professional experience, only one out of every 250 people can successfully manage their cash flow when using credit cards regularly. They are simply unaware of what they are spending. What about you? Can you try the "all-cash" method for two months and write down everything you spend in your notebook? Then compare it to your previous two months of credit card bills. Prepare to be shocked at how much you have saved!

**ME TIME**

## MONEY ENERGIZING TIME:
## Choose to Overcome Negative Emotions and Fear

As you internalize your reality, you will need to confront and shift your negative emotions. For this exercise, use single sheets of paper. Write down the one emotion or issue you most want to heal in this moment. Ask yourself, *What is my unmet need?* Eventually, something will pop. Whatever it is, feel the feelings as they come up. This is where the healing begins.

As you write, you are bringing your feelings about this emotion to the surface, shining light on it to feel and heal it. Then crumple up the paper and throw it away. Even better, burn it. By doing this, you are choosing to distance yourself from old, stagnant energy. This symbolic process allows you to internalize this dramatic event and feel what it's like to be done with negativity. By watching it burn, the emotion, fear, or limiting belief is symbolically removed from your life by choice.

I want you to try another exercise to help you come to terms with your emotions and fears. Turn off all the lights in your room. Lie down comfortably on a floor mat or on your bed, with your head and knees slightly raised. Relax your entire body with deep, cleansing breaths. Keep your hands folded across your stomach as you fill up your diaphragm and belly with air on the count of one and deflate it flat on the count of two. When you feel totally relaxed, focus on one emotion or fear: fear of failure, fear of success, anger, unworthiness—any emotion or fear you can pinpoint and identify as a problem for you. See it, feel it, know it, and blow it out and away.

As you inhale, visualize that you are inhaling a cleansing, white light; let it surround you, inside and out. Then blow it out, visualizing the darkness leaving your body. Continue with the breathing until you feel clear. This might take you a few times or multiple days or weeks, working on only one emotion or issue at a time. Rest assured; it will work. Choose to allow yourself the space and time it takes to dissipate these fears.

## MONEY ENERGIZING TIME:
### Learn to Make Wise Purchases

**ME TIME**     We all have decisions to make. The question is, are you making the wisest choices? Once you remove the judgment of "good" and "bad," you will find decision making becomes easier, less risky, and feels safer. It's empowering to make "wise" choices. Please note that the W.I.S.E. decision-making model I am about to explain works equally well on *things* you might purchase or *experiences* you might encounter. When concentrating on living authentically, the life experiences you invest in are far more important than material things. It's the memories and experiences of a life well-lived that people cherish and remember.

By making wise decisions each day and staying in the moment, you will be able to cut back on many impulse or ill-advised purchases. Wise decisions free up valuable financial resources that you can put towards things you authentically desire. Below, the acronym W.I.S.E. is laid out to test your emotional connection to spending. Once you practice these four steps on a regular basis, this approach will become second nature.

## The W.I.S.E. Decision-Making Model

**W: WHY** Why do I want this? Is it just temporarily satisfying an emotion, resulting in an impulse purchase? Is it something I really need? If you answer with no or "just because," it will not be a wise choice. Contrast this with another answer, one where you feel a very clear and meaningful resonating response from your inner self. That lets you know this is a wise purchase.

**I: INTENTION** Does this thing I want to buy today get me closer to what I really want in my life? Does it fill or support an intentional desire? Does it move me closer to my true intentions? If it doesn't, you're on the wrong track. Don't buy it.

**S: SAFE** Do I feel safer or have less anxiety when I think of purchasing this item? Or does my feeling of anxiety or depression go up because this does not fit my goals? If you have any anxious or uncomfortable feelings when thinking about a purchase, it's not a wise decision. Choose the safer route and keep your cash in your wallet. Choosing to buy things or experiences should always give you a peaceful or grounded feeling.

**E: EVOLUTION** Will this purchase help me evolve toward the financial reality I want to create? If at first you don't get a clear answer, meditate on it. If you're still in your head and thinking about weighing the pros and cons, it's not a wise choice. If you can't see clearly how this acquisition will move you along, then back off. Choose items and experiences that feel right.

## The Language of Your New Reality

Your thoughts aren't the only things that define and solidify your reality. Language is important. The words you choose to express your beliefs also shape your existence. Your vocabulary can either rob you of abundance or shower you with wealth. Do you limit yourself when you talk about your finances? Do you say things like, "Oh, I could never afford that," or "That's way too expensive for me"? Why deny yourself an abundant life?

My thought is that if talk show hosts and movie stars can make millions per year, why can't I? Why can't you? We all can if we choose to. There's plenty to go around. The first step is to select the appropriate language and actions to manifest what you want. The point here is that you become the words you speak. By saying out loud what you actually want to create, you draw experiences into your life.

Next, pay attention to how you respond to yourself and others. How do you speak to yourself? Most of us are nicer to everyone else than we are to ourselves. We should never criticize ourselves, since we get more than enough of that from the world around us. Once we manage our own self-talk, the next task is to not allow anyone else to criticize us in any way. Negative loaded language is all around us, but it's our choice as to whether we allow it or not. People tend to diminish compliments as if they are not deserved. This is particularly true for Generations X and Y because of their upbringing. No one was ever singled out for failing, and everyone received a trophy or a prize. As a result, individuality disappeared. Suddenly the goal was to become a member of the pack and be accepted and liked by all.

The words we use, the way we treat others and ourselves, and our surroundings all contribute to our well-being. If you don't react positively to someone or people don't bring out the best in you, stop spending time with them. This next exercise will teach you how to be more considerate and kinder to yourself.

## MONEY ENERGIZING TIME:
### Talk Nice!

**ME TIME**    There are enough people all around you who are quick to critique, so it's very important to speak nicely to yourself. We can choose to change negative, habitual mental patterns with physical strategies. Start with making your self-speak something positive, not a reiteration of what others say to you negatively.

- ♥ When you speak to yourself, are you self-judging?
- ♥ Do you call yourself names?
- ♥ Do you belittle yourself?
- ♥ Do you run the same debilitating script so often that it makes you want to scream?

Select one specific thing you do or say to yourself that you want to stop. For one woman in her 30s, it was racing thoughts about what she felt she "shoulda, woulda, coulda" done in her past or what she needed to do in the future. Be mindful of how you speak to yourself and decide what you will change this week. Making only one adjustment at a time will help make it a more permanent, internalized change.

Decide on a physical reaction you will use whenever you find yourself doing the behavior you wish to change.

A man in his 40s realized that he called himself "dummy" whenever he did something he didn't like. "You, dummy, you," he said. He decided to self-correct, and from then on, whenever he thought or said the word "dummy," he put his hand up like a stop sign. By the end of the first day, he caught himself simply on the sound "duh." On the second day, he almost stopped himself from even thinking "duh," and by the third day, it was not an issue.

When my "shoulda-woulda" client was "shoulda-ing" herself on the old, non-stop repetitive thought track, she stomped her foot as a signal to cut it out. My friend wears a rubber band around her wrist for this reason. When she feels her anxiety getting the best of her, instead of verbally attacking someone, she pulls the band and snaps it on her wrist. This snap disrupts her natural response and changes the way in which she reacts to stressful situations. Simple solutions like this cost no money and can genuinely positively impact your life.

It is simple to decide what will work for you. Maybe it's taking a step forward or backward, clapping your hands, or saying, "No more!" The physicality of the movement helps you break habitual mental patterns. I know a woman who taught herself how to stop driving herself nuts and wasting precious brainpower simply by snapping her fingers at any mindless self-punishment. There were a few remissions, usually brought on by stress or lack of sleep. "Then I simply reminded myself to snap it away," she told me. It's truly amazing what great things we can accomplish for ourselves when we are our own priority.

## What's Your Number?

Another choice you should consider is your career path. Think about your job and your employer. Is your current job the right one for you, or is it time to move on? Let me relate a cautionary tale about the world of work that will give you some perspective. My friend Frank's boss is constantly intruding into his life when he is not at work. When he is at home playing with his kids, if his iPhone dings, he's expected to answer calls or emails. He can't even work out at the gym to release stress without being interrupted by work issues.

Frank is also raising a family as the sole income provider. He grew up on food stamps at times, but today makes a hefty six-figure income, which would lead most people to think he is a big success. But he hates his job. "What's your number?" I asked him one day while he was complaining about work. "What are you talking about?" he asked. "What's your number before you decide to finally shift and move on?" When I first asked him this question two years earlier, his number was $10 million. In other words, once he hit a net worth of investments of $10 million, he would pull the plug on a job that was killing him on a soul level.

After about a year and a half, I asked him again, and he reduced his number to $7 million. Today he's decided that $5 million will provide him with what he needs to live his optimum lifestyle. Every day, I meet men who are tired of providing for their families at the expense of their souls. Men are starting to stand up for themselves, choosing to earn the incomes they want, but not at the expense of their well-being.

I'm happy to report that Frank has transitioned to a great new job. He is also working with a personal life coach and healer to help him comfortably evolve while continuing to make a good salary. Remember, it's not an all-or-nothing scenario. It's a transition and a process. Allow it to happen. Don't be limited by thinking you have to stay in any given job, especially when it no longer provides you with what you need.

## CHARLENE:
# Breaking through Limiting Beliefs

Limiting beliefs can be conscious or subconscious. On a conscious level, these are ideas you have learned from your own experiences with others to make you think you can't or shouldn't do something because it's out of your reach. In one of my seminars, Charlene, 50ish, said that growing up in the 1970s she used to watch *The Carol Burnett Show* with her grandmother. One night she bravely said out loud, "When I grow up, I want to be just like her, doing comedy on television."

"Hah! You? Like Carol Burnett? Very funny," her grandmother snorted. That comment stuck to Charlene like glue, making her doubt her own dream for many years, until her grandmother died. Then, getting up the courage to write out her act, she took it to an open mike night in a New York City club, and despite her lingering self-doubts, she went for it and performed. She was a hit, and within a month, she became the emcee of that club, with a new career ahead.

Limiting beliefs can be not only on the experiential level, they can also exist on the historical, energetic core, genetic, and soul level. Genetically, these can be patterns passed down from generation to generation and repeat themselves because we teach the next generation how to respond. For example, one pattern passed down through the generations was, "You have to work hard to survive," and another was, "Your job is not done until the prior generation is dead."

I was not conscious of these patterns until I worked with a healer who really zoned in on them and helped me see exactly how they played out in my life financially. For generations, my family was comprised of hard workers, at the cost of living in the present moment. They provided the income at the cost of their souls. I can trace my family lineage through this limiting belief.

Charlene came to me knowing she wanted to shift, but didn't know how. This showed me her limiting beliefs were rooted in the subconscious. If she were conscious of it, she would have already shifted. There are many times we need to bring subconscious limiting beliefs to the surface and clear them.

## Breaking Away from Our Parents' Mindset

These are the most common words associated with limiting beliefs: *I can't, I won't, I don't, I am not,* and *others might not.* Limiting beliefs are often comprised of positions held: *Men don't cry. Women should put their families before work. Airplanes are dangerous.* Today we know these tenets are outdated. In fact, the opposite is often the case.

My own limiting belief was that I had to work hard to survive. One of my lifestyle coaches told me I needed to reduce my efforts to increase my results. This sounded bizarre. I was hardwired to be "effort-based." I watched my parents, aunts, uncles, grandparents, and all of my role models work so hard that I thought that was the only way to function. There was pride in working hard and shame if you didn't.

My belief was that about 40 percent of my success was thanks to God and the Universe, and the remaining 60 percent came from my own hard work. But I decided to consider the point my coach made and shift. I needed to put more energy into manifestation to create results versus working harder. The way I achieved this was to open myself up to more spiritual opportunities. I set my intentions but detached from the outcome. I trusted everything would be orchestrated by powers beyond myself, shifting my balance to 80 percent spiritual and 20 percent hard work.

By working hard to survive, while operating under my limiting beliefs, I encountered another issue: my need to control everyone and everything around me. Whenever a change occurred, the feeling of needing to control things played out in my life because I was fearful of not getting my way, which stems from my childhood. As the second of 12 children, I depended upon being in control to survive. If I created scenarios that were predictable, I could manage the chaos of living in a three-bedroom house with 13 other people and a dog.

Always trying to control everything definitely zapped my energy, but I no longer need to do that now I'm a grown-up. I am physically aware that when I go to work, my "fight or flight" response system races to the forefront. Nervous energy takes over, and a huge lump forms in my throat. To counteract my limiting belief attacks, I visualize the outcome I want and repeat my affirmation: "Success beyond my wildest dreams comes to me with immediacy, grace, and ease."

I learned a few years ago that choosing adventure over control gives me the chance to naturally detach myself from my fears. It has taken me a good deal of time and attention to leave the "control freak" persona behind and open up to my increased consciousness, which taught me to shift from being reactive to choosing intentional responses.

## MONEY ENERGIZING TIME:
## Turn Your Passion into Reality

**ME TIME**     I want you to do another exercise. Write down your answer to this question in your notebook or journal: what things would you like to do but feel you'll never have sufficient money to make happen?

Don't be shy or edit yourself. Next to each item, write down the specific reason you think you don't have the money you need. For example, let's say you answered that you've always wanted to rent a villa in Tuscany for a month. Perhaps the reason you think you can't afford it is something like this: "I have one child in college and one in private school. I don't make that kind of money."

Now I'd like you to revisit each reason you've listed and reframe them to be more positive, using affirmative language. Make it something actionable. Life is too short to waste time with negativity. Focus on *can* instead of *can't*, *will* instead of *won't*. That way, you'll be a lot closer to living your ideal life. (See figure 7.)

| | |
|---|---|
| Can't | **Can** |
| Want | **Like/Desire/Wish** |
| Should | **Would/Could/Can** |
| Try | **Do or Do Not** |
| Hope | **Trust** |
| No more "buts" | **Use "and"** |
| No fault/blame | **Take Responsibility** |

Figure 7: Affirmative Speak

Here are some additional examples of negatives reframed as positives. (See figure 8.)

| | |
|---|---|
| I can't leave my job. | I **can** be happy in my career. |
| I want a bigger house. | I **desire** to buy a home that suits my family's needs. |
| I should stop using my credit card. | I **can** get what I want using the cash that I have. |
| I try to stop spending. | I **do not** want financial drama. |
| I hope I'll be able to retire one day. | I **trust** I will retire comfortably. |
| I could stop giving money to my kids, but... | I can help my kids out **and** teach them fiscal responsibility. |
| I'd have more money if they stopped raising taxes (blame). | I use creative tax strategies to reduce taxes owed **(take responsibility)**. |

Figure 8: Speaking in the Affirmative

## MONEY ENERGIZING TIME:
# Gratitude Goes a Long Way

**ME TIME**    I want to share a moment of personal vulnerability. When I was at the height of my debt and income was sporadic, my mentor, Bob Lyman, called me into his office for a chat. My financial situation was overpowering me and affecting my work. I had student loan debt of over $40,000, credit card debt over $8,000, car debt of $27,000, working on full commission, with no salary, while trying to learn a whole new business. From that day forward, even weekends, he mandated that I tell him five things I was grateful for, or else I'd be fired.

Of course, he turned out to be right. I was playing the victim role to a tee, and this was his simple and effective way to help me shift my focus to the positive things in my life. Teaching myself how to write down my grateful thoughts every day, and then report them back to him, shifted my consciousness to a more positive outlook. This was one of the greatest gifts I ever received.

I remembered seeing an *Oprah* segment where she interviewed Sarah Breathnach, author of *The Simple Abundance Journal of Gratitude*. Oprah said that every evening before going to bed, she writes down five statements of gratitude. My days are so jam-packed I can't remember if I ate lunch, but I do know it's powerful to keep a record of the daily gifts that life provides.

I sprinkle my gratitude statements throughout my day and find that it helps everything I do. Sometimes I am grateful for something as simple as looking in my bag and finding a little umbrella when a sudden shower hits. It can also be as big as gratitude for giving birth to a child. Some days I'm grateful for a warm meal, others for a great night's sleep. With a little practice, you'll find that gratitude comes easily and often. It's certainly not a chore of any kind. Keep it light. Send a quick thank you message by text or email to others, or even to yourself, when you feel the urge. Have fun with this and make it part of your daily routine.

One journal I keep is filled with cut out and pasted portions of thank you cards other people have given me over the years. Their beautiful messages put a smile on my face. When I'm having a bad day, I just pull it out to read, and it instantly shifts my energetic vibration. I also always try to remember to say thank you to the Universe for the little things that people do for me. Once you master daily acts of gratitude, challenge yourself to find something to be grateful for when you're in a difficult situation. For instance, while you're stuck in traffic, be thankful you have a car. If you arrive late to your destination, give thanks that you got there safely. By doing this, you're recognizing what is positive in the situation and giving it power. The more positive experiences you give thanks for, the more gifts will come your way.

## Keeping Your Options Open

When it comes to advancing at work and finding your happy place, this next story shows how powerful your mindset and intentions can be. Matthew, a single man in his 60s, was working as an adjunct professor in the English department of a major university. A policy change mandated that every adjunct working in the English department needed a master's degree in English. Unfortunately, his master's was in industrial engineering, so he was let go from his position teaching public speaking, which he had enjoyed for 12 years.

One week later, he received an e-mail from an administrative assistant within the business school at the same university, asking, "Can you teach a course in business communication?" "Absolutely," he responded. "I've inquired about teaching that class for at least the past five years, but was always told that two professors had it locked up."

"True," the woman said, "but one of them is retiring, and the other is teaching a new course. The department chair is holding a meeting tomorrow at two o'clock to speak with two new adjuncts, but I told her I thought you'd be really good. She said she would consider you if you could send your resume over to us by five o'clock today."

Matthew had not applied for the position but suddenly his name was on the list. He also found out that the administrative assistant had happened to deliver Xerox copies of some handouts in the middle of one of his presentation skills workshops. She was impressed by his skill and the reactions from the students. When the department chair found out Matthew knew a lot about teaching presentation skills and public speaking, he was given three classes to teach in the business school, including his dream course. The other two new adjuncts, who both had advanced degrees in business management, were only given one class each.

This illustrates that the Universe knows how to bring things together much more quickly and easily than we ever do. When that happens, our job is to take the opportunity and say, "Absolutely, yes! Thank you so much!" Matthew did not hesitate or mull it over. He was surprised but pleased—and smart enough to ride the wave into a new position.

## Doing Right by Yourself Will Feel Good All Over

The sports adage, "no pain, no gain," does not apply when it comes to your emotional health. If you are in emotional pain, something is wrong. A need is not being met. Get out of this situation you are in. Make a change. One of the most important parts of the PACT method is to enjoy your new reality as you create it. Your enjoyment will help raise your energetic vibration even higher. People will be attracted to you with job opportunities, money, new relationships, and much more. Whatever you desire will be yours because you are in the driver's seat.

Changing years and years of patterns and less than optimal choices is not an easy task. Loving and treating yourself with grace will make the transition easier. Remember, you are worth it. The world needs you and your authentic gifts. Physically, it takes more energy to frown than to smile. By applying practical and simple techniques and doing small, positive steps, it's possible to create huge forward strides. This chapter has been jam-packed with everything from the power of intention, to choosing the right experts, to watching your inner talk, to how to make W.I.S.E. choices. Through it all, I want you to understand the critical importance of making new choices. Now it's time to integrate everything you've been learning and take action. The "T" in PACT is coming right up.

 ## Financial Meditation

*I am so grateful for my financial achievements. I am powerful standing on my own. I provide beautifully for myself and my family and accept full credit for my accomplishments. I have everything I need. I choose to change. I accept me. I am enough. I am worthy. And I am proud of my choices and my ability to choose what is best for me. Yes, I can!*

# CHAPTER 7

# T: TAKE ACTION

*Action is the foundational key to all success.*
*~PABLO PICASSO*

Congratulations! You have made it to the "T" in PACT. This is the point where we focus on compartmentalizing your financial numbers to make them more palatable and manageable in order to put money's energy to work for you. It's the stage where you connect your reality to your dreams and your desires and let them become your new reality. We have a tendency to become overwhelmed by the big picture. When something seems daunting, or we really want to avoid it, breaking it down into pieces will make it more doable.

In this chapter, I will address the final tactical steps of the PACT process that is designed with the goal of creating everlasting changes in your financial situation. Let's start off with something I know you will like. As you begin to pay off your debts and plan for the future, you need to find ways to reward yourself so you can stay motivated.

I tell clients to try to think of something they've wanted for a while, but just couldn't see how they could possibly afford it. Then I show them how they can make it happen. Once they experience how it feels to achieve it, they are hooked on the process.

## The Magic of Staying Motivated

For years, Jacob really wanted to experience going to a sports fantasy camp. His wife, Audrey, thought it was a huge waste of money because *she* didn't value it. But it was extremely important to Jacob. He had been working really hard for a few years, paying down their house maintenance debt. When it was finally paid off, I said to him, "When you get your next bonus, you need to go to that camp." His wife sighed, but he lit up like a Christmas tree.

I'm happy to say that when his next bonus came, he went to camp. You would have thought he won the lottery. Audrey valued debt payoff. After getting what he wanted, Jacob agreed to scratch her itch. They felt motivated to get even further out of debt by allocating more money monthly to pay off their mortgage within the next 10 years, at which time they both will be 47 years old. That's freedom. The ball and chains are coming off for them. They love it and are living life comfortably in the meantime.

Dynamically, in their relationship, Audrey always did the ultra-responsible thing, while Jacob wanted the next fun adventure. Neither path creates long-term happiness. She needed to have more fun in the present moment, and he needed to clean up his past debts. Today she's having more fun and adventures, and he feels more relieved with less debt. In the end, they're better partners to each other by collaborating.

Here's why this technique is so powerful. The left side of the brain might fight you for a logical answer, but you can rely upon your right brain to enjoy a creative treat. Is it a new outfit? A spa retreat? Maid service? A weekend in the mountains? Ignore the left brain's insistence on being completely logical and enjoy your indulgence.

You've earned it! As a result, your heart will sing. The massive smile on your face will create even more motivation and give you the energy boost to reach for your next level of happiness. In this next exercise, it's your turn to brainstorm.

## MONEY ENERGIZING TIME:
## Begin with Self-Examination

**ME TIME**   The responses you provide to the following questions will reveal trends in stages. Don't try understanding it while doing it; just record every answer to each question and then go back through the list, adding details as they come to you. These answers will change over time as you shift your energy and position, making it important to revisit this exercise at least once a year. Since you are evolving, so will your answers. For example, if you are uncomfortable with the amount of money in your retirement fund, begin brainstorming creative options to build it up or perhaps consult with an expert in the field for more options. Or you might find that gifting and donations have become important to you. Decide how you would like to do that, what it will mean, and what amount you will use.

Consider your answers to these questions in light of what you discovered about yourself in previous chapters. Recognize possibilities to bridge from one side, your current reality, to your desired future. As your intuition begins giving you hints, write them down. These clues and observations will provide great jumping-off points for the rest of the financial exercises coming up.

# FINANCIAL SELF-EXAMINATION
## Finances and Your Debt

- Do you want to dramatically reduce or eliminate your debt? If so, how do you want to prioritize paying it off?
- How are you ridding yourself of any residual shame, blame, guilt, and judgment you have surrounding your finances?
- How much money do you want in a short-term emergency reserve? Having three to six months of readily available cash is recommended. Does that amount make you feel comfortable? Does that align with how long it would take to get a new job in your field of expertise? Do you think this is feasible?
- At what age do you no longer want to have to make a mortgage payment?
- What amount of debt is tolerable for you? Has that tolerable debt level now become just part of your lifestyle so that you always seem to have that same amount, year after year?
- How do you feel about the debt you are carrying? Does it zap your joy?
- Do you know the exact amount of your debt?
- What is the interest cost to you in actual dollars? We identify with dollars, not percentages. It's important to know the actual dollar amount being spent on interest alone.

## Children and Family

- Are you allowing your children to drain your cash flow? Do you choose to continue allowing them to do that? Are those the values you want to teach them?

- ♥ Do you need to create healthier boundaries with your children and the way they spend your money?

- ♥ Are you, or will you be, fiscally responsible for your parents? If they require long-term care, are you willing to pay for it or become the caretaker? Will your finances allow for this?

- ♥ Do you want to pay for your children's college educations? If so, do you think they will attend an in-state, out-of-state, or private university? How much of that cost can you bear?

- ♥ If you have no children, are there people in your life—nieces, nephews, godchildren—who are really important to you? Do you want to contribute anything to their college funding?

## Spending and Expenses

- ♥ Are you spending money in ways that are relevant to you today?

- ♥ What are the periodic expenses that throw your cash flow for a loop? Do you want to create a plan for the surprises or known annual expenses that occur?

- ♥ What do you want your financial story to be?

- ♥ Is gifting important to you—with your time or your money?

## Wealth and Retirement

- ♥ What's your number? How much is enough when building your wealth? Is it based on income or asset level or both?

- ♥ How do you feel about your retirement savings level?

❤ Are you minimizing the taxes you owe with the investments you currently hold? If you're not sure, do you want to consult with a tax specialist?

## Paperwork and Products

❤ When was the last time you had your legal documents updated or put together? Is it time to take a look?

❤ What are the current financial products you have?

❤ Do the financial products you hold today support your current financial intentions?

❤ If you have life insurance, does that satisfy your needs? If you're not sure, go to my website, www.jmcwealth. com, for a needs analysis.

❤ Are you aware of what your employer covers for disability insurance? Keep in mind, if your employer pays for your disability insurance premium costs, then the benefit is taxable to you. Meaning you will go home with less money than you think. Will that net tax amount meet your monthly expenses? If not, do you want to consider a supplemental disability plan? Is it important to you?

With these answers in mind, you are ready to begin structuring your new financial reality.

## Restructuring Your Financial Picture

Everyone should use these six categories to break down their finances. Business owners need six for yourself and six for your business. (See figures 9 and 10.)

1. Past: debts
2. Present: current cash flows, cash in and out
3. Future: wealth accumulation
   a. Short-term future
   b. Mid-term future
   c. Long-term future

| Past | Present | Future |
| --- | --- | --- |
| Debt | Cash Flow | Assets |

Figure 9: Financial Timeline

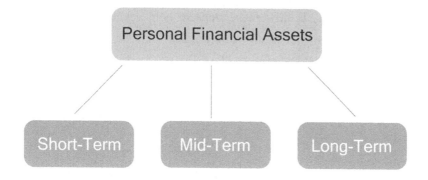

Figure 10: Your Personal Financial Intentions

The first step is breaking down your financials into these separate categories: debts, current cash flows, and income you want to create in your future. To help you do this, I have included a series of step-by-step exercises to help you. Please note, I do not use the word "budget." When asked to figure out and stick to a budget, we act like teenagers. Some of my clients literally shut down just at the thought of creating a budget. We like our flexibility and don't want to be restricted in any way, or we rebel with overspending. Instead, I suggest we recognize the reality of our bottom line and cash flows in order to assign amounts to different areas, savings accounts, and investments, all to support our intentions.

## MONEY ENERGIZING TIME:
## Working out Your Financial Past

**ME TIME**    Focusing on our past finances can create anxiety, making it all the more important to find peace and harmony in the present moment. It's sobering to open up all the envelopes, list our debts, and accept the reality of the totals. Follow these steps to help acknowledge the reality of your money and finances, and be prepared to take action. (See figure 11.)

| Debt with highest interest rate first | Rate % | Current Balance | Current Payment | Minimum Payment |
|---|---|---|---|---|
| 1 | | $ | $ | $ |
| 2 | | $ | $ | $ |
| 3 | | $ | $ | $ |
| 4 | | $ | $ | $ |
| 5 | | $ | $ | $ |
| 6 | | $ | $ | $ |
| 7 | | $ | $ | $ |
| 8 | | $ | $ | $ |
| 9 | | $ | $ | $ |
| 10 | | $ | $ | $ |
| 11 | | $ | $ | $ |
| 12 | | $ | $ | $ |
| 13 | | $ | $ | $ |
| 14 | | $ | $ | $ |
| Totals | | $ | $ | $ |

Current - Minimum = $

Figure 11: List Your Debt

1. Prioritize your debts from top to bottom with the highest interest rate on top of the sheet.
2. Write down the minimum monthly payment on all of them, except the one that has the highest interest rate.
3. Take the total of the actual payments you make monthly on all debts and subtract the minimums on all but the highest rated one.
4. Take the answer from #3 and pay that large, lump sum every month on the highest interest debt until it is gone.
5. Once the first debt is paid off, take that lump-sum monthly payment and apply it to the debt that is next in line, the second highest interest-rate debt.

Repeat this cycle until all the debt on your spreadsheet has been completely wiped out.

Once you have paid off all accumulated debt (congratulations!), you can shift from financial *defense* to financial *offense*. Here's how: take that full payment of, say, $700 per month and allocate it to your wealth-building to fund your intentions. Do this at three levels: short-term, mid-term, and long-term, simultaneously. Put these all on automatic deposits so you don't even need to think about it. You won't miss the $700 because you've been living without it for so long, and now that money is working for the future you create by choice. Don't let old patterns from your subconscious creep up on you to play havoc with your money. Refer back to the financial exercises in chapter 5 to remind you of what you don't want to do and review your snapshot of today's reality as you keep adjusting and improving the overall picture. This will shine the light and make you aware of what is or is not in alignment with you in real time.

## The Benefits of Strategic Debt Reduction

Why have I asked you to pay off the highest-interest debt first? The answer is simple: it is the most expensive money you have going out. Human nature is to pay down the largest balance first, but the real issue is how the interest is being compounded. My system will quickly and easily reduce the invisible money, the interest you are paying for the privilege of "borrowing" their money. In reality, paying down the largest debt first keeps you trapped longer, and the financial drama never ends.

Follow the system exactly as I mapped it out to receive the greatest emotional and financial rewards. Paying off that first line of credit will give you the motivation to keep going. It is empowering to step out of the debt trap. Once you pay off the first line of credit, take that payment (say it was $400 per month) and add it to the debt next in line. If the minimum payment was $50 per month and you add the

$400, your new total, $450, is going to the second-highest interest rate creditor on the list.

Remember earlier when we talked about rewarding yourself along the way? Using the example where you paid off the first debtor and you've moved on to the next one on the list, consider making a $300 payment to the debt each month and assigning the other $100 for an intentional financial decision. It could be a reward for yourself, or you could save for a big reward in your future. This extra money can be assigned to your short-, mid-, or long-term financial intentions. You can choose to pay down all of your debts—student loans at 6 percent interest, car loans at 1.99 percent, or mortgages at 3.75 percent—using this same system. The happiest people I know don't carry a lot of debt. Once we get the motivation to get out of debt, we usually want to maintain that feeling forever.

In many ways, living debt free is like losing weight. I don't know anyone who enjoys being overweight, but we keep eating too much of the wrong foods or not exercising. With both money and food, we need to get out of our own way to create the body and life we truly want. Your job is to evaluate the emotional versus financial to decide which aspects of your life are most important to you. What feels right for you?

## Current Cash Flows

If your challenge is making ends meet or it never feels like you have enough cash to pay the bills, the solution is to stop using debit and credit cards for at least six months to a year. Doing this will help you internalize what you spend and makes money a real, physical thing, not some unfathomable entity. Once you start consciously knowing what you are spending your money on, your priorities will immediately shift. When you start recognizing the rewards of living the life you want, you won't want to return to the way it was. I've met people who make $40,000 annual income and have a more satisfying quality of life than those with $500,000 annual income.

For some reason, our collective belief system is that if you don't have a high income, you don't have a high quality of life. That's not necessarily true. Yes, having more money is nice, but what's most important is what you do with the income you make. The key is to pair up the cash inflows to create intentionally lower outflows. Don't just try, *do*. Don't just hope, *trust*. This is a very personal choice. The power to create the quality of life you desire is in your hands.

## MONEY ENERGIZING TIME:
## Setting up Your Own Bucket System

**ME TIME**     Pry open the door to dreams and energize your life $10 at a time. Systematically drop what money you can into buckets. It doesn't matter how small the amounts are. Here's the formula that works best: a portion goes toward paying down debt, a portion supports your current expenses and lifestyle in the shorter term, and a portion goes into the future, which is broken down into short-term future, mid-term future, and long-term future. In order to grow from where you are planted, you need to realistically use the various buckets to your best advantage. Start with an amount you are going to save and allocate that across the three levels. When you receive chunks of money, such as a raise, bonus, tax refund, or an inheritance, use the same allocation method.

## A Quick and Easy Checklist:

a. One-third pays down debt.

b. One-third saved for future spending: Car! Vacation! House!

c. One-third into future buckets for wealth accumulation. For example, spread $75 each month across each of your financial timelines: $25 into a short-term savings plan, $25 into a mid-term investment or account, and $25 for retirement or the long term.

The key is to work with the dollars you have. Begin today with $10s, $100s, or $1,000s.

## Coming to Terms with Emotional Spending

My client and friend Samantha called to ask if she should sell some of her Apple stock to pay off her $10K credit card debt. She is not a person who is comfortable owing anyone money. She doesn't carry a mortgage, owns her house outright, has no car debt, and no lingering student loans. However, she had accumulated significant credit card debt and was bothered by it to the point that she was considering selling stock she bought for $2,500 in 1998 that was now worth $25,000. She made a really great investment in Apple years ago, and, yes, it was smart to pay off the debt with a portion of the stock gains. This would return her to her more comfortable debt-free status.

But before she did that, I asked her to try and understand what created the overspending in the first place. Samantha acknowledged that she was in an unusual situation. She processed her father's death by overspending, which helped her feel better in the short-term. She was distraught by all of the debt she had created, and now she had the means to pay it off. A few months later, she called to say she was seeing a grief counselor to deal with her emotions around her father's death in a healthier way.

In contrast, many of us who carry debt are not conscientious purchasers. Instead, we have made spending an unthinking process. To become a conscientious purchaser, I'm right back at my recommendation to use cash. Chances are slim that Samantha would have handed over $600 cash for a jacket or $414 for a pair of shoes with cash, unless she really loved them. Big purchases tend to be the ones that throw us for a loop, but smaller nickel and dime costs really add up, too. Using cash reminds us of our spending habits better than swiping some plastic.

I know this only too well. A married couple had a power struggle over whose purchases, his or hers, were having a greater impact on their cash flow. He insisted that his large purchases coincided with when his bonuses arrived and that he paid everything off right away. But then he began itemizing the monthly variable spending, tracking her nickel and dime purchases against his large purchases. After six months of careful watching, the numbers were almost identical. This surprised him, but it was a powerful lesson. No doubt about it, use cash and you will become a more conscious spender!

## MONEY ENERGIZING TIME:
## 10 Quick Ways to Boost Your Cash Flow

**ME TIME**   Regardless of income, anyone can tweak their spending habits and energize their life with the money they have. Even the smallest changes quickly add up to improvements in the big picture. These are my Top 10 quickest ways to increase positive cash flow in your life. How many can you start to implement today?

## #1. Reduce Automatic Credit Card Billings

This includes cell phone plans, gym memberships, and any other ongoing bills. One client called a competitive car insurance company the day before her automatic payment transaction to check if she really could save money by switching. Sure enough, the savings were significant and were directly deposited into her new "vacation fund."

Another black hole is forgetting to cancel memberships or unwanted expenses that are automatically billed to your credit cards. When you plug up those holes, intentionally use that cash to fund your new and improved life.

## #2. Find Creative Solutions to Reduce Your Rent or Mortgage Expenses

Megan, late 30s, desperately wanted to remain in the three-bedroom condo she bought while earning a six-figure income. Then she started her own business and her income became more sporadic. To balance things out, she rented the two larger bedrooms to roommates and kept the smallest one for herself. With their rent payments, her monthly out-of-pocket housing cost was only $300. These simple measures allowed her to keep living in her beautiful home while growing her new business.

In contrast, Amanda was out of work for two years and accumulated $45,000 in credit card debt and decided to move into her parents' basement apartment. Within one month, she shifted her financial energy to proactive rather than reactive and landed a new dream job that doubled her previous income. I helped her devise a new game plan to pay down her debt and purchase the car she needed for her new job.

## #3. Compartmentalize Your Money

This is a golden go-to strategy. When one debt is paid off, such as a car payment, allocate that car payment to go automatically from your checking account into a "new car" account monthly.

## #4. Increase Your Deductible

Once you have saved $1,000 in an emergency reserve fund, contact your car insurance carrier to raise your deductible up to $1,000, from the standard $250 or $500. Then proactively take that monthly savings of approximately $30 per month and add it to your emergency fund. Create your own insurance plan by making interest on your money as opposed to giving it away.

## #5. Others Can Contribute to Your Retirement Fund

If you are buying a new residence, consider the option of having someone else contribute to your retirement fund, especially if you are behind in your planning. Add up the numbers in your current cash outflow for mortgage payment, real estate taxes, association fees, and maintenance. Research to see if the cash outflows match what you could receive in a rent payment. If you can at least break even, rent out your old place as you move into your new place. This is a creative way to help build your financial future.

## #6. Weigh Your Weekly Expenses

A client realized that her largest weekly expense was for gasoline. "I am so tired of feeding the pump," she said. "I don't know much about hybrid cars, but I'm going to find out everything I can, to save money and contribute to a healthier environment." She selected the model she wanted and called every dealer in the state to negotiate the best deal. She wound up purchasing a slightly used hybrid, which cut her gas costs in half. Find your highest bill and try and reduce it.

## #7. Consider Using Public Transportation

If you live in a major city, try limiting how many times you use taxi cabs and car services. These costs can average about $300-$400 per month and could be cut by taking the bus or subway. If you are adamant about keeping your car in a big city, parking becomes an added cost. Do your research. There are great apps to help save money in this regard. I personally use the "Spot Hero" app to find the least expensive parking garages in Chicago. I'm sure there are many similar apps for other cities.

## #8. Shoring up Your Grocery Bill

Eating healthy is very important. We shop at Whole Foods or, as some people call it, "Whole Paycheck." However, it's possible to shop at even the priciest grocery stores and stay within your desired cash outflows. One way to get around extra costs is to buy the fruits and veggies that are in season, in abundance, and—most importantly—on sale. You can shrink your grocery bill by purchasing the weekly featured items and shopping the perimeter of the grocery store, where foods are typically less expensive and healthier.

## #9. Set an Amount for Your Weekly Pocket Money and Always Pay Cash

If you tend to do a lot of "little spending," decide on your weekly allowance for coffee, groceries, gasoline, lunches, etc. Take cash out every Monday, and when it is gone, so is spending until the following Monday.

## #10. Adjust Giving or Gifting to Your Current Financial Circumstances

It is always admirable to give to those who are more in need than yourself or to give to charitable or religious organizations. I encourage everyone to adjust that giving based on a percentage of income, instead of actual dollars. Many of us have taken pay cuts since 2008 but are still gifting the same dollar amounts. It is important to take care of ourselves and then take care of others to make a much bigger impact in the world.

## Impacting the Larger World

When I spoke before the United States House Budget and Finance Committee in Washington, D.C., someone asked me, "How do we get Americans to save more money for their own retirement?"

"You're asking the wrong question," I responded. "We as a country are barely making our day-to-day cash flows. We need to first address the debt issue in this country." I told the assembly that it's too easy to declare bankruptcy and reinstate credit. There needs to be more stringent consequences or more compelling reasons for people to change their behavior. There are very few cases where bankruptcy was not self-induced by overspending and insufficient savings.

In reality, the amounts of currency that are going to pay down debts far exceed what previous generations invested in or needed for retirement. We need to address and resolve the debt issue by educating adults and children on fiscal responsibility. By addressing debt problems, the money currently going to debt payment will resolve the immense challenge that the majority of people have: insufficient retirement savings.

For reasons I will explain in chapter 8, Generation Y, also known as Millennials, born between 1977 and 1995, will need to save 15 percent more than prior generations to retire at the same levels of income. We must address this now, from an individual and personal level, and not wait for the system to fix it.

### JULIE'S GEMS:
## Gifting so That Everyone Wins

I'll never forget the day my nephew Matuka said to his mom, "Aunt Julie is on TV! She grew up in the same neighborhood as me, and that means I can be on TV, too, someday." I gave him hope that he, too, can do anything he chooses. This experience marked the day I elected to open up college funds for all of our 40 nieces and nephews (and still multiplying) to reinforce that college is possible—regardless of where you grow up.

For every birthday and Christmas, they each receive a $50 direct deposit into their college fund. Not all of them are very excited about something they can't touch or use today, but it gives them hope to think about their future education, and it's something I greatly value. This is just one example of how you can feed your soul while helping others along the way.

If you can't afford financial gifts, then volunteering your time and energy, or sharing a skill or a sympathetic shoulder, is just as important. Doing good feels great and raises your energetic vibration. When you are happy or feel or express love, scientists have proven that the energetic vibration of your body is at the highest energetic frequency possible for a human being. While giving to others, don't forget about your own immediate family. My sister reminded me, when I set up education funds for my nieces and nephews, that I also have four children of my own who need college funds.

It was a reminder to keep all of my authentic passions funded and that I need to be hitting all cylinders to be true to myself. I know that when I energize my money with what I value, it will work out. At nine years old, my son Timmy has a nice chunk in his college fund. I chose not to increase my lifestyle expenses as my salary grew, and I do not live on all of my income today. I chose to live below my means to make my future, and that of my children, easier. The decision to save for their educations feeds my heart.

## MONEY ENERGIZING TIME:
## Making Your Dream List Work for You

**ME TIME**    Now that you know yourself so well, why not make a dream list, just as Michael did when he wanted to see Notre Dame's Fighting Irish play football in South Bend, Indiana? Stop and ponder the things you've always wanted to do that haven't happened yet. Feel the excitement welling up inside as you write them down and begin to make them happen. When you fulfill your first round of dreams, move on to the next one. When your lists are in place, create a timeline that will chart your accomplishments six months, a year, and five years down the road.

## Make a Date

If you'd like your financial PACT to be more of a partnership with your spouse, consider initiating "financial date nights" to make sure you are both on the same wave length in regards to funding and prioritizing your mutual goals. At least once a year, my clients would rewrite their Dream List for their family together. They address these five subjects: financial, personal, spiritual, family, and career. It really helps to hear each other's take on how they're doing.

When we take a look back at the previous year's list, we are thrilled to see how many things we've accomplished together. We tune in to our hearts and ask ourselves if the things left open from last year are still important. We only keep them on the list if they remain a priority. Each time we repeat it, the process renews itself.

## Living Your Ideal Financial Life

It is not enough to just *plan* to clean up your financial past and transform your present cash flows, all while breaking down your future wealth accumulation into the short-term, mid-term, and long-term levels. You need to actually do the things that support what you want to create. This is where you must return to visualizing your intended life, as my clients did at least once a year.

Remind yourself of the steps in the PACT process. Choose to be the person you admire. Proactively change your vocabulary, maintain healthy boundaries, meditate, exercise, and sometimes just go play.

Create space for your personal growth by shedding toxic relationships, eating a clean and healthy diet, and clearing the clutter out of your home while earning a tax deduction by giving to charity what you don't want or need. Most important, prioritize what you truly want to fund. It's your money, and it's your responsibility, privilege, and joy to use it to your benefit.

## MONEY ENERGIZING TIME:
## Take Care of Your Future

**ME TIME**    The PACT system provides you with everything you need to establish the future of your dreams through your finances. An important part of PACT is the "bucket system," which we have referred to and used in different ways in other sections of this book. As you know, I suggest that your future needs be broken down into short-term, mid-term and long-term categories. Begin by determining the total dollar amount you already have invested in the future. Next, consider how much you can save monthly on an ongoing basis from this point on. The last task is to break down how much money should go into *each* bucket monthly.

In saving for your short-term future, consider how much you currently have in an emergency reserve fund. Then look at your long-term category and determine how much money you have been able to save and lock in for your retirement years, taking into account the various plans you have contributed to at work or on your own.

Now, you can consider any other long-term accounts or assets that do not fall into these short- or long-term categories as part of your mid-term savings for the future. This includes money set aside in college funds, brokerage accounts, mutual funds, exchange-traded funds (ETFs), and any real estate you hold other than your primary residence.

Once you have written down your overall current amounts, you will be able to see how well balanced they are in relationship to each other. How much money to contribute monthly depends upon which buckets are very low and which are already quite healthy. It makes no sense to say that you will take your monthly allotment and distribute it in equal amounts across the board to all three buckets. If one category has been neglected and needs to get a greater share of your income for a certain period of time, do it.

I suggest that you determine a planned allotment for each budget and review it at least once a year. That way, you can create a balanced relationship among all three future buckets, which will help to ensure your accumulation goals are met. Continue regularly reviewing your savings strategies to reflect changes in your circumstances or any new desires you might have for your future.

## Enjoying the Benefits of PACT

Now that we've reached the end of this fourth step, what used to be a chore—agonizing over the best interest rate, reconciling your bank statement, and cleaning up your credit cards—has gradually become a joy. Why? *Because you are now connected to your source of wealth.* You own it and know what it means to take care of yourself and your money. You probably never imagined that accepting full responsibility for your cash inflows and outflows would be so liberating. I see these revelations occur all of the time with my clients and with others who have gone through my seminars and webinars or heard me speak.

Through PACT, you will experience the human elements of financial well-being. You have internalized how to live a healthy financial existence, while feeding your soul along the way. By now, it should be clear that PACT is an ongoing process, like life itself. The good news is that as you learn PACT, it will become part of your DNA. In the process, you will be building your financial knowledge and self-confidence daily. The best part is that you will have your life back, the way you want it. Today, tomorrow, and the path ahead are full of your dreams coming true. Be proud of yourself for creating your own safe space where you can be you. By following your own decisions and choices, you can hold true to your personal boundaries, with stopgap measures firmly in place.

One client says the way she can tell that she's falling back into her old ways is when she starts pulling her credit or debit cards back out. She decided to take the only credit card she has left and put it in her freezer, where it stays for a true emergency. The debit card remains in her pocketbook as her security blanket, but she keeps it in a separate envelope with these words printed across it in thick black letters: *Stop and think. Pay cash or do without.*

One thing I know for sure is that instituting automatic contributions to savings or investment accounts has already changed your life. It's amazing what a difference it makes when you know the money is put aside to pay taxes and you don't have to worry if an appliance breaks down—you are covered! Depending upon what you really like to do, automatic withdrawals, along with creative planning, mean that thanks to that vacation savings account, you can get away for an unplanned weekend whenever you want. Simultaneously, you'll be building wealth through your personal accumulation goals that can finance your children's college funds, a second home, or retirement income. You'll be doing it all with your emotional and financial numbers in balance. Join me now in the next chapter to see how to live an ImPACTful life based on who you are and the life stage you're at.

Welcome to the financial freedom you so richly deserve!

 ## Financial Meditation

*I live my dreams. What I visualize and feel for myself are drawn to me, forming an empowering and energizing picture. I am creative, innovative, intelligent, and resourceful. I choose to live with the conviction that life offers me infinite possibilities. I surprise myself daily and receive and accept more real wealth and abundance every day. Thank you.*

# CHAPTER 8

# LIVING AN IMPACTFUL LIFE

---

*Happiness lies in the joy of achievement and
the thrill of creative effort.*
~FRANKLIN D. ROOSEVELT

---

Each generation has its own characteristics and financial fingerprint, which impacts everyone from that era. Tom Brokaw described those who grew up during the Depression as "The Greatest Generation" in his book by the same name. These were the men who fought in World War II and the women who went to work to keep the country running. During the war, whether on the battlefield, in factories, or at home, both genders learned to live in the present. At times, it was difficult to survive day-to-day, much less think of the future. Yet they endured.

In general, they were really good cash flow managers, maintained an amazing work ethic, and accumulated much of the wealth that exists today, which continues to be passed down to subsequent generations. Unfortunately, too many of their heirs are letting this abundance slip right through their fingers. If you have not figured out how to create or even hold on to money yourself, it is highly likely you will ultimately lose it.

The Greatest Generation's retirement planning was typically taken care of by employee pension plans. They didn't have to worry about diversification of portfolio or their money running out like many do today with 401ks, 403(b), and other employer retirement plans. The money just got deposited every month into their checking account, like social security checks, and that's what they had to spend that month. Sadly, many seniors from this generation have regrets about things they wish they would have done differently with some of their other hard-earned money.

This chapter explores how current generations view their finances and their world and how the PACT process can be applied to their lives today as they reach their own milestones.

## Baby Boomers

Baby Boomers are those born between 1946 and 1965, following World War II. Boomers overall have earned amongst the highest household incomes of any other generation to date. They grew up in Depression-era households with parents who saved for that rainy day and who possibly died on, or from, their jobs. This created an interesting dual reality: some Boomers saved for the future, but their counterparts, the flower-power hippies of the 60s and 70s, believed that "tomorrow is promised to no one, so you may as well live it up." This segment either didn't save at all, or saved very little, compared to other Boomers. In the end, some Boomers have viable retirement plans while others do not. Some have pensions that will last them through retirement, while others were not so lucky. Some started out with pension plans, then converted them into less costly alternative programs, with the employee making the majority of contributions.

This generation aged at the same time that the corporate mentality changed, with companies putting a new focus on efficiencies, profits, and downsizing. This radical turnaround from valuing people to prioritizing technology has, in large part, created the fear-based mentality that drives our economy today. Simultaneously, abundant credit access has allowed people to spend now and pay later, so why worry? Boomers today are caught in a multiple bind of insufficient savings, which causes them to drain whatever funds they have too quickly, and the outside pressures caused by distressed economic growth globally. They are personally laden with debt.

The only way to retire comfortably under these circumstances is to come up with creative and innovative solutions. You want to make sure that your portfolio is working at its best levels possible. You want to cut back on your spending, and you may possibly want to redefine retirement—which might mean continuing to work part-time in some capacity. Emotionally, many Boomers are not ready to retire when they reach the typical retirement age of 65 or 70. They still want to be plugged in to society. It doesn't have to be all or nothing. One creative solution I'm seeing is, instead of going for a pay raise, some Boomers are negotiating a shorter work week. This provides a better quality of life while they remain fiscally and mentally fit.

## Generation X

Generation X, commonly referred to as "Gen X" or "Gen Xers," includes those born between 1965 and 1982. Gen Xers, who are age 34 and above, have average retirement savings of less than $55K. Considering that people are living longer and healthier lives, the $55K some manage to save won't go very far. Fortunately, there is time still for those people to build up their savings.

This generation loved their parents' lifestyle but didn't want to wait or work for it in the same way. They attended colleges of their choice and racked up considerable education, car, and credit card debt. With easy access to credit, they bought and sold homes. Now many are shaking their heads in confusion, wondering why they made those expensive choices and wondering how to fix it.

Gen Xers are the current sandwich generation, financially strapped under compounding debts and raising their children, while simultaneously having concerns for their aging parents. Strong work ethics have served this group well, but it's time to get paid what you are worth. Women, are you willing to only be paid 77 percent—a well known fact that President Obama emphasized in his 2014 State of the Union address—of what your male counterparts earn? Of course not! One thing you can do for yourself right now is to reserve a portion of all raises, bonuses, and tax money returns for your well-being and financial future.

## Millennials

Those known as "Millennials," "the Millennial Generation," or simply "Gen Y" were born between 1982 and 1996. There are 88 million Millennials, larger than the Boomer generation. Some social researchers say this label extends to those born in the early 2000s. There are Millennials whose parents are Boomers, and others whose parents are Gen Xers. Millennials don't like debt and try to only do jobs they are passionate about. These are out-of-the-box thinkers who do not believe life has to be linear. This generation is expected to change jobs 16 to 20 times over the course of their working years. This comes from their experience of spending vast amounts of money for college and graduating without the jobs or careers they expected to find to give them satisfaction and also to adequately pay down their steep debt—all while watching their families suffer from economic duress.

One young woman I worked with faced her financial picture realistically by joining with friends in the same boat. Together, they were a staggering $300,000 in debt. They chose to buy into a business whose operations they could potentially fix up with their combined skill sets, turn around, and eventually sell for enough profit after taxes to pay off their enormous debt. Instead of allocating 25 years to paying back debt, they chose to pay it all off in five years, a quantum leap.

This generation believes in infinite possibilities. Think about it. You graduate from college and discover that everything is a mess. There's the sheer weight of your debt, the financial struggles your family is going through, and your lack of trust in Wall Street doing right by anyone but the already rich. What happens? You decide to apply the perfect mix of creativity and innovation to this difficult situation. With today's technology, anything is possible. The challenge for Millennials is to trust the system enough to pay for your lifestyle and also save for retirement.

However, to retire, this group needs to save 15 percent more than their parents because they receive lower incomes after graduation, and their high amount of debt chews up their income. Much of this discrepancy between generations stems from the economy's sluggish state of low growth or no growth between 2000 and 2018, while Gen Yers were growing up. Over the next 15 years, the market is expected to grow less than it did in previous generations, according to the April 2015 issue of *Forbes*. This has made Gen Yers ultra conservative. As poor as their savings rate is, 41 trillion dollars will be theirs when their parents pass away. They need to prepare now so they will be able to hold on to this abundance and not let it slip through their fingers. To have the financial freedom they desire, Millennials need to create a long-term retirement plan, along with tax planning and financial planning.

# PACT for the LGBT Community

One goal we all share—or should—is to travel the best path financially in ways that bolster our assets and benefit our most important relationships. Emily, age 40, and Molly, age 37, had been together as a committed couple for several years when they began considering marriage. They came to see me and asked for my help because they were making plans for Emily to sell her condominium, in which they were both living, to buy a home together.

Molly worked in the fashion industry, and Emily held an executive position in a real estate company engaged in city planning. They wanted to develop a working financial plan that would allow them to become equal partners in the relationship, even though Emily made twice Molly's salary. It was important to them that they both contribute fairly, but also proportionately, to their vacations, their home, and daily living.

Now that they are no longer limited by law and can marry, the PACT process helped them consider whether or not getting married was worth paying more in federal income taxes. Did the emotional aspect make up for the cost of additional tax money going out of their pockets?

PACT also helped them think through other upcoming decisions, such as, what would happen if they chose to have children, married or not? What last name would their offspring have? When married, would either of them change their name to create a family name? Which one of the two would physically give birth to a child or children? Who had maternity benefits at work? Whose health insurance would include the child? In addition, if not married and still filing taxes separately when they had children, who would claim them as a tax deduction? They certainly had a lot to consider and appreciated the clarity and simplicity of PACT to lead them on their way. Emily and Molly are now living in their own home, raising their 18-month-old daughter, and have hyphenated their last names.

## PACT for Recent Graduates

During your first few years following graduation, whether it's graduation from high school or college, when you begin working, you will set the tone for your future. What intentions do you want to set with the money you make? This is a critical period because it's when many financial habits are set in motion. You want to make clear-headed choices with full intentions behind them.

Kristen, age 22, graduated college with student loan debt, found a job with a decent income, and decided to live on her own. Some would argue that she should have lived at home with her parents for as long as possible and used all of the extra money she saved to pay down student loans. This is something that makes total financial sense, but sometimes dependency upon family is not the best move. Kristen's decision meant it would take longer to pay down her debt, but, in the meantime, she would enjoy living independently—which could bring her to a higher plateau as she climbs the ladder of success.

By following PACT, recent graduates can create a sound roadmap to work towards their goals, moving them where they want to be, in spite of an average $27,000 in student loans.

## Time for a Raise

Congratulations, graduate, you're about to get the biggest percentage pay raise of your life thus far. What is the wise choice here? How do you want to allocate it?

Let's say your monthly student loan repayment is $1,000, along with your other expenses for groceries, entertainment, gym membership, car, gas, and insurance, with a net income of $2,000 per month after taxes. You have just been notified that you will receive an after-tax pay raise of $1,000. The suggested PACT route is to simultaneously clean up your past, while you live in the present moment and plan for the future.

But what does this mean in terms of raw numbers? Let's break it down. You can allocate an additional $325 per month to pay down the student loan debt and spend an additional $325 per month towards things like travel, a car, or saving to buy a house. And, yes, this is spending and not saving. Too many people convince themselves that this is actually saving, but in reality it's not. You are saving to spend, which means it's spending. It is rather easy to fool ourselves when it comes to money, isn't it?

Lastly, divide the remaining component of new income of $325 per month into three financial future areas: short-term emergency reserves; mid-term savings for an advanced college degree in five years or other accumulation wealth goals; and long-term retirement savings. Congratulations, once again. You have funded your intentions!

## Funding Your Intentions at Every Age

This is a story I tell often because it shows how you can fund all your intentions and create your best life and that some people can even do it from a very young age. My brother John was my youngest PACT client ever. He is 12 years younger than I am, with eight siblings in between our birthdates. He was 11 years old when he had his first paying job, and I was just beginning my career. He came to me because he wanted to know what he should do with his money. At the time, I suggested that he save half for the future. At only 11, John had the foresight to listen to me.

A year later, he had another question: "Is there something more I can do with my money? Julie, you told me to put away half, and I've been doing that, about $150 a month, but it doesn't make much interest in a savings account." His entire life, he watched as our siblings went off to college. He paid attention to the concerns and complaints about accumulating student loans. At age 12, he knew he didn't want to be in debt. He decided to put $50 into a general savings account, $50 towards a college fund, and $50 toward retirement. He fully understood that he could create whatever he wanted.

In retrospect, this was an early incarnation of the PACT philosophy that I have spent many years fine-tuning. John continues applying PACT to his life today. When I meet with him and his wife, both in their late 20s, I see that they are well on their way to creating a healthy and beautiful life together based on their dreams and desires, without creating debt. They paid cash for their beautifully classic wedding with all the trimmings, with money left over. So impressive!

## The PACT Process for the Newly Married

You're totally pumped; you are getting married. Be sure to have the "financial conversation" *before* you move in together or tie the knot. It's time to get financially naked. I cannot tell you how many people think they have an "idea" of their romantic partner's financial situation but really have no clue.

This advice brings us back to setting healthy boundaries. Each of you need to share your personal debt details: the good, the bad, and the ugly. Stay cool and calm; simply collect information. Be sure to hold the safe space of non-judgment for whatever the other person says. Try not to be shocked or dismayed, particularly if he or she reveals a pattern that you recognize to be identical to one of your parents' tendencies. Maybe that behavior was something you wanted to run away from but inadvertently attracted. This happens quite often. We are attracted to people who exhibit familiar behaviors.

To effect change, you need to set the stage for how your marriage will operate. When sharing information, both partners need to feel safe and respected. Choose to let this first major money conversation be the beginning of a beautiful, collaborative marriage. Make your way through the PACT process as if you are a married couple, which you are planning to be. Respond to the questions on an individual level to find your voice; then compare notes with your future partner. This helps to insure your authentic voice will be heard by the other party. It's important you both choose to participate and buy in to the process. Find bridges or commonalities on both of your lists. This will give you the fundamental ingredients to create your future, sound financial household.

 ## The PACT Process When Buying Your First Home

When selecting your first home, buy the place you see yourself living in for 10 or more years. If you plan on moving in five to seven years, consider securing a 15-year-fixed mortgage so you actually pay down principal. With a 15-year-fixed mortgage, you will have paid down about half of the debt within seven years, rather than paying off mostly interest on a 30-year-fixed product. This actually allows you to get ahead and not keep spinning your wheels.

There's an old line that many mortgage brokers always use: "You need flexibility in your cash flow." They are pushing your fear buttons. Don't fall for it. Decide, up front, the outcome you want to create and then select the mortgage product that supports it. There are times when a variable rate mortgage makes sense, but be careful. Watch out for those costly second-stage "balloons" that can pop up and burst your carefully laid plans. If you are unsure which product to buy, go to www.bankrate.com, an online resource that helps you run the numbers and calculate different options.

There are 10, 15, 20, 25, and 30-year-fixed products available. There are also 5, 7 and 10-year ARM (Adjustable Rate Mortgage) products and "interest only" deals where you do not pay down the principal. Oh, and don't forget, all of these products can be sold with a 10, 15, 20, 25, 30-year amortization schedules. (Many people don't know what this part is about, but it's key to your mortgage planning.) Look at which option will give you the best rate and if what you need to pay down in principal fits your personal preferences for debt payoff. You can choose a five-year ARM if you know you plan to move in five years. Typically, this is done to secure lower, and more flexible, payments.

But is that all you want out of the situation? Ask yourself what principal you will want to have paid down by the time you move. Often ARM products are based on 30-year-fixed amortization schedules. This means you hardly pay down any principal whatsoever. Return to your PACT lessons: *pick the one that feeds your intention.* Since we know money is energy, you must choose the money flow that supports the energy you want to create in your life.

If you are buying your first home, isn't it wonderful to know that when you are 40-45 years old, you will no longer have to make mortgage payments? Find a way to make the larger payments. Mortgage payments must be submitted monthly, on time, and should never be used to pay towards other debts or expenses. People who inherently want to keep their homes will find a way to do it. Decide at what age you want to no longer pay this debt and set the track in motion with your desired financial and emotional outcome. Position yourself to "be lucky."

 ## The PACT Process When Expecting

Most people think starting a family will be a huge burden on your cash flow. Guess again! A lot of the initial outlay is in planning for the baby to come, money spent on the furniture, educational toys, and clothing—which additional siblings can eventually use. I don't see children really as a major addition to other expenses until (and if) baby number three comes along. This is due to lifestyle changes you make when you become a parent. Your lifestyle changes drastically with the birth of your first child. The money you used to spend on extracurricular activities suddenly goes to diapers, formula, and car seats, shifting one expense for another.

If both parents will be working outside the home, expenses that need to be considered are day care, babysitter, live-in nanny, or au pair. In reality, financially, it can be cheaper for one person in the couple to stay home as opposed to both working and paying for full-time child care. One client couple vehemently argued this point with me. This was a reality they did not want to accept. Neither parent wanted to be the one staying home. Yet, every month, they lost money from this arrangement. This is another example of the fact that most financial decisions are not 100 percent about the fiscal side of the equation.

## The PACT Process for your Children's Education

Education clearly has become one of the largest expenses parents have to plan for. The first rule is to decide what is important to you. Would you prefer to plan to pay for your child's in-state tuition, out-of-state tuition, or a private, Ivy League school tuition? You pick. Project the costs and begin saving. If your child wants to go to a school that is more expensive than what you have budgeted for, you will have to let her know it is up to her to pay the difference from her own savings, or in the form of scholarships, student loans, or a combination.

There is high demand for higher education. The United States has one of the strongest educational systems in the world, one that draws students from around the world, which makes it all very competitive. Once you as a parent finish paying off your own student loans, I recommend you put that same payment into a separate savings or investment account that is specifically set aside as eventual college money for your children or future children. This is what I started doing seven years before my first child, my son Timmy, was born. With

PACT, you can balance your goals and not put everything into one big bucket.

## The PACT Process When Facing Divorce

What it comes down to is this: can you work out your challenges in your marriage, or is it time to move on? Fifty percent of marriages today end in divorce. No one gets married with the intention of divorcing, yet it is often a messy and heart-wrenching process. If you make the decision to end your marriage, know one thing for sure: you are not going to get rich fighting through the divorce process. People waste thousands of dollars in attorney fees that could be avoided if both parties would agree to collaborative mediation. Not only is it less stressful, since the ordeal of fighting each other can negatively impact your health, but it also costs far less money.

Certainly there are exceptions. If huge amounts of money are at stake, the final result might be worth the expense of high-powered attorneys. In any case, we all need to protect what is ours, especially for the future of our children. Using PACT will provide you with the structure you need to work through each step by helping you put your desires and goals foremost and reinforcing them with a clear focus on your bottom line and future needs.

# The PACT Process as You Plan for Retirement

The closer people are to thinking about retirement, the more important it is to put PACT to work. There are many creative choices. In the 1970s, about 50 percent of all Americans were subject to mandatory-retirement regulations requiring that they vacate jobs by a specific age, which was usually age 65. In 1986, Congress abolished mandatory retirement by amending the Age Discrimination in Employment Act. Some professions are exceptions. However, retirement today can often be defined in any way you wish. It is not unusual for seniors to continue working into their 70s, 80s, and beyond. Irving Fields, 101 years old and a former band leader, plays piano at a number of his regular New York City gigs. People find creative ways to be active and contribute, often in fields they haven't tried before. Steve Jobs nailed it when he said, "Let's go invent tomorrow as opposed to worrying about what happened yesterday."

Actual abundance has little to do with the specific dollars. It is about the quality of life with the income and assets available. Using PACT, you can evaluate what is working in your life and what needs adjusting. Does your current home fit your wants and needs? Do you need to downsize or can you stay put? Are you in an area where you have easy access to groceries and necessities? Retirement is a new beginning. You have a blank canvas. Paint it however you wish. It may be your last adventure. Make the most of it.

## What Is Real Wealth in Retirement?

There are some gender differences at play when people plan for retirement. Men, in general, tend to view wealth—how much money they have—as success. Women, on the other hand, think of success more in terms of security. But how should we see real wealth in retirement? According to Michael Finke, PhD, CFP®, and a professor at Texas Tech University, the number one factor in retirement is good health. Dr. Finke's research has found that having a portfolio of up to about $3.5M makes people happier in retirement, but having more than $3.5M becomes a burden.

Age and physical condition also impact happiness. Today's retirees, between the ages 65 and 80, tend to travel more than past generations and have more mobility in general. Spouses are also extremely important, especially the quality of the marriage. People in healthy marriages live longer, happier lives. The goal in retirement is to reduce stress while striving for health and happiness.

Dr. Finke's research also found that maintaining a positive relationship with adult children is important. Interestingly, seniors living within 10 miles of their children are less happy in retirement than those who live further away. Yet many seniors downsize their living arrangements and deliberately move closer to the children and grandchildren. The distance is not nearly as important as the relationship.

Plan ahead for what feeds your soul. Try to have as many household things as possible taken care of by others. Sometimes the simplest parts of life can be the most difficult and certainly time-consuming. If anything becomes too much, don't hesitate to ask for help. Dr. Finke's research showed that those who have a guaranteed income, receiving monthly checks from annuities, pensions, and Social Security, feel more secure. He also found that those with guaranteed income live, on average, five years longer than those without a reliable income.

You will need to decide where and how to allocate large lump sums from 401ks in order to continue providing you with the income you need from your principal nest egg. Be aware of financial decisions made on the distribution of income from your portfolio. If you have questions, consult a professional or ask your current expert to run some simulations for you. Make decisions and choices from a position of knowledge and understanding. Living abundantly is about far more than just the numbers.

## Why Not Do It Now?

Don was a widower at age 68, and he had set aside $1.5 million for his children. After his wife died, he felt as though his own life had ended. I repeatedly asked, "Isn't there something in your life you've always wanted to do? Do you have any regrets?" As I asked that question, I saw a small smile form at one corner of his mouth. "What just flew through your head? What is it?" I was so curious. The smile got bigger as he confessed, "I have always wanted to go to law school."

I pointed out that he had the tuition covered by earned interest from his nest egg, still leaving the principal for his children. He quickly listed all of the reasons why he couldn't achieve his dream: "I'm too old"; "People my age don't go back to school"; "I don't know if I could keep up with the work." My response was, respectfully, "Blah, blah, blah." He looked shocked. "Well, it never occurred to me that starting this whole new order now was an option," he responded.

A few months later, he walked into my office and presented me with his acceptance letter. "I'm going to law school," he announced. He went, passed the bar on his first try, and began practicing law at the age of 72. He worked full-time at his new profession, with great joy, until age 84. No one is ever too old or too young, too fat or too thin, too rich or too poor, to go for what he truly desires. No excuses accepted!

# KEEPING YOUR PACT GROWING

*It is important to remember that we are energy and that energy cannot be created nor destroyed: it just changes form.*
~**ALBERT EINSTEIN**

**D**ear Readers:

I hope you agree that it's been a lovely journey together through these pages and the PACT experience. Let's end our time together by summarizing your take aways so you can continuously grow your financial success and find more freedom and happiness.

In this book, I have shared my very best professional advice on financial planning, savings, investments, and insurance. This includes the following observations from my personal and professional experiences:

- ♥ Feeling + thinking = financial healing.
- ♥ Thinking includes dreaming big about your life and seeing that your potential truly has no limitations.

- Feeling is experiencing the emotions pulsating through your body and allowing yourself to visualize what it will be like living those dreams right now—so you *feel* as if they have already materialized.
- Express gratitude for the fulfillment of your dreams and give thanks as if they are already manifested—and they will!

PACT allows you the space to take a financial quantum leap, and the PACT process will walk you through the action steps you need to pull this all together.

## Be Proactive, Not Crisis Reactive

The day Brian and his wife walked into my office, he looked like he was in the prime of his life, but I was in for a shock. He had just been diagnosed with a rare cancer, and there was a 90 percent chance he would die within nine months. Brian and Scarlet had been fiscally responsible all their lives. They traditionally made prudent decisions, the business they owned was hugely successful, and they had a multi-million-dollar estate. We discussed his diagnosis, and I encouraged him to go after his retirement dreams right now, despite the fact that it might not be the best timing.

Although he had no time to waste, he was still hesitant. He knew his dream project was not financially "prudent," so he wondered why I recommended going for it. It didn't make sense to him. I understood why he balked at it, but I explained that he really should go after his dreams. He would be spending the equivalent of only one and a half years of the earned interest on his total investment portfolio. His principal would not be touched. He left the office, and I wasn't sure if I would ever see him again, but soon, to my delight, I heard he had proceeded with his plan.

A year later, Brian returned to my office, looking vibrantly healthy, telling me all about the completion of the renovation. He grinned as he announced he no longer had any trace of cancer in his body. His lifelong dream was to completely remodel his childhood home, and he made it happen. The project cost him hundreds of thousands of dollars, and he was thrilled to be hands-on with every detail, even though the house would not sell for half of what he spent, given the location. The project was a labor of love, which provided him with an incredible sense of personal achievement and likely saved his life to boot!

Can these financial principles cause miracles? In this case, they were certainly part of the solution. A number of factors contributed to his overall healing process, including medical care, nutrition, exercise, and an overall positive outlook. But sometimes reframing our paradigm can lead to creative solutions as we strive to unlock our authenticity and fulfill our dreams. Brian's story is an example of how everything can work out when we create trust. Brian's actions and overall attitude provided him with a new lease on life. He used his money wisely to fulfill his dreams. His own energetic vibration increased to such a degree that he began attracting an abundance of pure health and happiness into his life. That is what I want for each and every one of you.

 ## Financial Meditation

*Clear your mind. Take a deep breath in and out. Continue breathing deeply. Allow the tension in your body to release. Visualize your ideal life. See the pieces fitting together. Acknowledge your part as creator of your own reality. Celebrate your conscious choice to accept your own authenticity. See yourself taking action to turn your dreams into your new reality. Smile as you think about your many achievements and give thanks for your blessings. For it is you, in collaboration with the God/Universe,*

*who is now creating your world, every day, for the rest of your wonderful life. How very wonderful life is.*

# ACKNOWLEDGEMENTS

I am who I am for all those that had the courage to love me enough to tell me what I needed to hear—not what I necessarily wanted to hear—to make me the best version of myself. I am forever grateful for those who have been in my life in the past, those who are in my daily life in the present moment, and those yet to be in my future.

To my parents, my big bunch of siblings, and my aunts and uncles, and to others, thanks for the lessons along the way which have allowed me to flourish! To my business partner and brother, Mark Murphy, and the JMC Wealth Team, both past and present, I am so grateful for all of your support to help me manifest my dream to financially heal our world.

To my supportive surrogate family, Bob Lyman, Jennifer "Pip" Brennan, MaryAnn Roti, David Wells, Oly Schalow, Karyn Pettigrew, Carrie Hansen, Anne Emerson, Marie-France Collin, Dr. Brian Foley, Vicki Milligan, Lisa Phillips, Barb Belcore, David Ji, Nancy Liebman, Travis McKay, Dierdre Morgan, Billy Rapka, Michael Gilardy, and Panache Desai, my journey could not have been as rich without all of you in my life. Much love to you and yours!

Thank you to my support team who helped manifest this book using their unique gifts: my longtime friend and editor extraordinaire Judy Katz, who always knows what I want to say and how to say it best. Thank you also to Simone Graham for editorial assistance to blend together both sides of my work, the financial and spiritual worlds. And thank you, Lindsay DiGianvittorio, for asking me such detailed questions, forcing me to really dig deep to clearly articulate my process in a relatable and digestible way for the world. This book would not be the same without each of your gifts you shared with me.

For the souls who have transitioned to help on the other side, my grandparents, Grandma and Grandpa Erxleben, thanks for teaching me the practicalities of life that have helped me stay grounded in my work to bring PACT to the world. Grandma Murphy, thanks for giving me the strength and courage to do it in a classy, elegant, safe, and loving way.

# RECOMMENDED RESOURCES

## Favorite Websites

- ♥ Panache Desai, www.panachedesai.com
- ♥ Anne Emerson, www.thepassionatejourney.com
- ♥ Dierdre Morgan, www.deirdresinsights.com
- ♥ Kelly Howell, www.brainsync.com
- ♥ The Chopra Center, www.chopra.com
- ♥ DavidJi, www.davidji.com
- ♥ Dr. Richard J. Davidson, www.investigatinghealthyminds.org
- ♥ Stuart Hameroff, MD, www.quantumconsciousness.org
- ♥ Dr. Darren Weissman, www.thelifelinecenter.com
- ♥ Bruce Lipton, www.brucelipton.com
- ♥ Gregg Braden, www.greggbraden.com
- ♥ Heart Math, www.heartmath.org
- ♥ Carolyn Myss, www.myss.com

# RECOMMENDED READING

- ❤ *Sacred Contracts: Awakening Your Divine Potential* by Caroline Myss, Harmony, 2009.

- ❤ *The Power of Now: A Guide to Spiritual Enlightenment* by Eckhart Tolle, New World Library, 2004.

- ❤ *Secrets of Meditation: A Practical Guide to Inner Peace and Personal Transformation* by Davidji, Hay House, 2012.

- ❤ *Perfect Health: The Complete Mind/Body Guide, Revised and Updated Edition* by Deepak Chopra, Three Rivers Press, 2001.

- ❤ *Breaking The Habit of Being Yourself: How to Lose Your Mind and Create a New One* by Joe Dispenza, Hay House, 2013.

- ❤ *Discovering Your Soul Signature: A 33-Day Path to Purpose, Passion & Joy* by Panache Desai, Spiegel & Grau, 2014.

- ❤ *Feminine Lost: Why Most Women are Male* by Jennifer Granger, Weinstein Press, 2014.

- ❤ *The Biology of Belief: Unleashing the Power of Consciousness, Matter, & Miracles* by Bruce H. Lipton, Hay House, 2007.

- ❤ *Way of the Peaceful Warrior: A Book That Changes Lives* by Dan Millman, HJ Kramer, 2006.

- *The Turning Point: Creating Resilience in a Time of Extremes by Gregg Braden*, Hay House, 2014.

- *Wishes Fulfilled: Mastering the Art of Manifesting* by Dr. Wayne W. Dyer, Hay House, 2012.

- *The Law of Attraction: The Basics of the Teachings of Abraham,* by Esther Hicks and Jerry Hicks, Hay House, 2006.

- *I Quit, and Choose Work That Aligns with My Soul* by Karyn Pettigrew, KP Consulting, 2003.

- *You Can Heal Your Life* by Louise Hay, Hay House, 1984.

- *Heal Your Body* by Louise Hay, Hay House, 1984.

- *The Tapping Solution: A Revolutionary System for Stress-Free Living* by Nick Ortner, Hay House, 2014.

- *Entrepreneurial Strengths Finder* by Jim Clifton and Sangeeta Bharadwaj Badal, Gallup Press, 2014.

- *StrengthsFinder 2.0* by Tom Rath, Gallup Organization, 2007.

- *The Body "Knows,"* by Caroline Sutherland, Hay House, 2001.

- *The Power of Your Spirit: A Guide to Joyful Living* by Sonia Choquette, Hay House, 2011.

- *Trust Your Vibes: Secret Tools for Six-Sensory Living* by Sonia Choquette, Hay House, 2005.

- *What You Don't Know About Student Loans Can Hurt You* by Ce Cole Dillon, Grave Distractions Publications, 2015.

- *The Art of Extreme Self-Care: Transform Your Life One Month at a Time* by Cheryl Richardson, Hay House, 2012.

- *Be Yourself, Everyone Else is Already Taken: Transform Your Life with the Power of Authenticity* by Mike Robbins, Jossey-Bass, 2014.

- *The Emotional Life of Your Brain: How Its Unique Patterns Affect the Way You Think, Feel, and Live—and How You Can Change Them* by Richard J. Davidson and Sharon Begley, Plume, 2012.

- *Happiness Genes: Unlock the Positive Potential Hidden in Your DNA* by James D. Baird and Laurie Nadel, New Page Books, 2010.

- *The Conscious Parent: Transforming Ourselves, Empowering Our Children* by Dr. Shefali Tsabary, Namaste Publishing, 2010.

- *Sacred Powers: The Five Secrets to Awakening Transformation* by Davidji, Hay House, 2017

# ABOUT THE AUTHOR

Julie Marie Murphy (CLU, ChFC, MBA, CFP®) has more than 24 years' experience as a CERTIFIED FINANCIAL PLANNER™ and is often referred to as a *financial healer* or *money therapist.* She is turning the personal finance industry upside down by redefining standard financial planning approaches and educating people about a new way of finding financial success, *following a process which starts from within.*

Julie's first book, *The Emotion Behind Money: Building Wealth from the Inside Out,* focused on really recognizing how emotions are entangled in our financial world and how to work through them in a healthy manner. She has helped at large, being seen on WGN Chicago, CNBC-TV, Lifetime TV, Oprah & Friends Radio, *The Wall Street Journal, Associated Press,* and more. Julie is the founder of JMC Wealth Management, Inc., in Chicago. She is also a motivational speaker and media expert on the topic of emotions and money.

www.jmcwealth.com
www.juliemurphy.com

Made in the USA
Monee, IL
15 March 2022

92271945R00128